Great Canadian CAKES

PAMELA STEEL

Prentice Hall Canada

A Pearson Company
Toronto

SF   0502

National Library of Canada Cataloguing in Publication Data

Steel, Pamela
  Great Canadian cakes

Includes index.
ISBN 0-13-033976-8

1. Cake. I. Title.

TX771.S744 2002   641.8'653   C2001-903679-5

ISBN 0-13-033976-8

Editorial Director, Trade Division: Andrea Crozier
Acquisitions Editor: Nicole de Montbrun
Production Editor: Catherine Dorton
Copy Editor: Karen Rolfe
Proofreaders: Sarah Weber/Dawn Hunter/Susan Broadhurst
Art Direction: Mary Opper
Cover Design: Mary Opper
Interior Design: Mary Opper/Julia Hall
Illustration: Doug Martin
Cover Image: Mary Berry/Dorling Kindersley
Production Manager: Kathrine Pummell
Page Layout: Arlene Edgar

1 2 3 4 5   WEB   06 05 04 03 02

Printed and bound in Canada.

ATTENTION: CORPORATIONS
Books are available at quantity discounts with bulk purchase for educational, business, or sales promotional use. For information, please email or write to: Pearson PTR Canada, Special Sales, PTR Division, 26 Prince Andrew Place, Don Mills, Ontario, M3C 2T8. Email ss.corp@pearsoned.com. Please supply: title of book, ISBN, quantity, how the book will be used, date needed.

Visit the Pearson PTR Canada Web site! Send us your comments, browse our catalogues, and more.
www.pearsonptr.ca

A Pearson Company

For my petite brioche, Amanda

Acknowledgments

This book was possible only with the help and generosity of many, many people across the country. Cooks, bakers, pastry chefs, farmers, food writers, home economists and scientists all shared their knowledge and recipes and allowed me to put together a book that represents cake baking in Canada today.

Some of these brilliant culinary minds have been vital to my work over the span of a few projects—and still they answer the phone when I call. For their wonderful generosity, I would like to thank Regan Daley and Daphna Rabinovich, who have both been sources of knowledge and encouragement. Many thanks go to Heather Trim, who also is kind enough to use her food-styling expertise to make me look good on media tours, Rose Murray, Mairlyn Smith, Dana McCauley, Micheline Mongrain-Dontigny, Johanne Pouliot, Steven Beyrouty, Joan Ttooulias, Edna Staebler, Pam Collacott, Chris Fenton, Lorraine Stevenson and *The Manitoba Co-operator*, Judson Simpson, Ellen Pruden and the people at Canola Information Service. I am indebted to Lucy Waverman, Emily Richards, Jo Marie Powers, Debbie Diament, Jenny Koniuk, Gaye Musselman, Nancy Wilson, Helen Steel, Jeannie Dunphy, Grandma Rockey, Jim Anderson, Nanna Rögnvaldardóttir, Nicola Stevens, the Alberta Barley Commission, Irene Wasylik, Miriam Schnee, Donna Hamilton, Mary Williamson, Rena Winter, Jo and Keith Walton, Aunt Ruby and Mabel, Mary Lou Harrison and her grandmother Foster, Jill Seward, Jane Langdon, Dawn Hallman, Joanne Leese, Kim Groomes, Sandra Post, J. Gail Phillips, Veronica Beer, Joan Lyddiatt, Simone Demers Collins, Dorothy Long, Sandra Cranston-Corradini, Trudy Patterson, Carol Ferguson, Margaret Fraser, Dufflet Rosenberg, André Théberge, Troy the Dessert Boy,

Donna Hamilton, Barb Holland, Monika Paradi and Barb Ackerman from the Cook's Place. Some of the recipes in this book first appeared in *President's Choice® Magazine* and were edited by Patricia Holtz and Sasha Chapman; I miss working with them both. Anne Hollyer from The Senator Restaurant contributes at least one great recipe to every book, and I thank her. Therese Taylor and everyone at the Women's Culinary Network have been a delightful resource; I used their directory to contact many wonderful food professionals from the Toronto area. The members of Cuisine Canada were also a tremendous help to me.

Many, many thanks to the whole team at Pearson including Nicole de Montbrun, Ed Carson, Andrea Crozier, Catherine Dorton, Karen Rolfe, Martin Litkowski, Jennifer Matyczak and Mary Opper.

I can never express fully the debt of gratitude I owe my family for their support and patience. To Bill, Nathan and Amanda, a thousand thank-yous. And finally, thanks to Jessie, Luke and Kayla Walton for keeping Nathan and Amanda occupied while I baked and wrote.

Contents

The Bare Necessities   1

Canada's Favorite: Chocolate Cake   19

Great Canadian Cakes

We are a nation of bakers. We bake pies and cookies, we bake breads and biscuits and we certainly bake cakes. Baking is a European tradition that sailed across the pond and adapted itself to our frontier. Canadians have, since the beginning of our nation, baked all manner of cakes. Tall butter cakes, layered with scrumptious fillings and buttercream, are our favorites and we wouldn't let a birthday pass without one. When we are born, there is cake; when we graduate, there is cake; when we wed, there is cake. We have coffee cakes and muffins for breakfast, snacking cakes and pound cakes for lunch and decadent chocolate espresso cake for dessert.

Cakes have not changed fundamentally in hundreds of years. Most are of northwestern European origin and are a variation of either butter cake or foam cake; others are more French in nature and rely on layers of meringue or dacquoise. Then there are the light, airy charlottes and mousse cakes that melt easily on happy tongues. Our Canadian flavors come through in the regional fruits we bake into our cakes and in the maple syrup we incorporate into our batters. No flour in the world equals ours, and our recipes highlight its special characteristics. Fresh Canadian ingredients call us to bake from scratch. Our sweet tooths demand to be sated, but with a balanced, complex flavor rather than with something overwhelmingly sweet.

There is more to cake than what's on the plate. So I've included a chapter devoted to the history of cake, another to the science of cake, and a third to cake decorating. During my research, I discovered that rudimentary cakes have been baked and eaten since antiquity and that the cake we know and love has been a staple at home and on restaurant menus since flour, sugar and chocolate became easily obtainable. As with all baking, science is important, and the baker who understands the process is likely to produce the best cakes. As for cake decorating, in "An Eye for Detail" I explain the equipment and ingredients necessary for turning a simple cake into a work of beauty.

My work has always been about celebrating the Canadian cook and baker, from the best professional kitchens to the warmest home oven, and that theme continues here. As in *Great Canadian Pies* and *Great Canadian Cookies,* the other books in this series, I have spoken to great bakers from all our regions. I have collected recipes for Reine de Saba from Quebec, war cake and partridgeberry cake from the Maritimes and good old saskatoon berry muffins from the west. From Ontario, there's niagara tipsy cake and elderberry chiffon cake, among many others.

I am honored to write this book. It is wonderful to speak with professional chefs, food writers, pastry chefs and home bakers from across this diverse land about something close to my heart: cake. It is a special gift indeed when someone chooses to share a recipe with me. As I bake, I feel closer to the originator of the cake. What a lovely group of people. Everyone has been so generous with their time, their knowledge and their recipes. This book was not really written by me, but by every cook who appears in its pages. These are Great Canadian Cakes.

The History of Cake

By the time Marie Antoinette admonished the people of Paris to eat cake if they didn't have bread, rounds of sweetened, leavened flour had been baked and eaten for centuries. In his *Oxford Companion to Food,* Alan Davidson notes that the word "cake" is possibly of Viking origin from the Old Norse word "kaka." However, to find the true beginnings of cake, we have to look to the beginnings of bread. A rough form of grains cooked on hot stones could be said to be the first bread, the remains of which have been found in many ancient sites.

Shall we say that to be cake, the bread must be sweetened and leavened? Honey-sweetened breads were consumed in ancient Egypt as early as the second century BCE, and ancient Greeks prepared a variety of cake-like products or "plakous." As for leavening, Romans were well acquainted with yeast by the second century CE, while northern barbarians were using the yeasty foam from beer to leaven breads and cakes. By the fourteenth century, literature provides evidence of great towering cakes, not only raised and sweetened but also elaborately decorated.

In the seventeenth century, European bakers had access to spices, dried fruit, chocolate and vanilla and, most importantly, sugar, which meant that gingerbread, fruitcakes, macaroons and even sponge cakes could be baked. Leaveners changed from yeast to well-beaten egg in the eighteenth century, and in the mid–nineteenth century, the home baker could begin to produce the light, soft cakes of today by using baking soda and baking powder. Inexpensive flour, sugar and shortening and improved ovens added to the popularity of cake baking. Northwestern Europeans were accomplished bakers, and brought their skills when they arrived to colonize Canada.

Mary Williamson of the Culinary Historians of Ontario writes that there is an abundance of early recipes from the earliest newspapers and periodicals, and cookbooks brought by immigrants. Some recipes used in British North America arrived directly from Great Britain. Others, whose origins can be traced to Britain, France, Germany and other parts of Europe, were brought by Loyalist cooks who left the Thirteen Colonies in the late eighteenth century. These same recipes spread to Ohio and other parts of the American Midwest at about the same time. Mary says,

> I have confronted Canadian food writers who glibly declare that spices were unheard of in the nineteenth century in this country, when in fact they were generally used from the very beginning of European settlement.

> Early nineteenth-century newspapers offered new brides basic cake recipes such as pound cake, dough cake, cream cake, clove cake and shrewsbury cake. The latter recipe appeared in most Canadian and American cookbooks up to the 1950s. Fruitcakes, sometimes called black cake, were eaten at all times of the year in the nineteenth and early twentieth centuries. They usually had brandy and/or wine in them, and a chunk of nutritious fruitcake could be tucked into a farmhand's pocket to fortify him for a day in the fields. Cupcakes and marble cakes were also popular.

> In *The Canadian Settlers' Guide* (1855) Catherine Parr Traill offers recipes for silver cake and golden cake, which the reader is instructed to bake at the same time because one uses 11 egg whites and the other the yolks!

Mary goes on to talk about the types of cakes and flavors being baked in early Canadian cuisine:

> Johnnycake [was very popular]. I have a lovely quote from 1842 from a traveling Englishman: "If a Canadian can keep up his supply of pork and pumpkin-pie, of molasses and sourcraut, of tea and Johnny cake—which he seldom fails to accomplish—he feels perfectly indifferent regarding those household conveniences which are not so eminently useful."

One early nineteenth-century traveler typified Canadians as "johnnycake eaters!"

Food Historian Jo Marie Powers asked students of a food and culture course to describe their holiday meals:

> Those whose ancestry went back to Upper Canada invariably had carrot pudding (often baked nowadays), which may have originated in Scotland. The Highlanders

had so little food that they sweetened boiled puddings with carrots and/or parsnips. It's possible that our Christmas carrot cake may be a remnant of that "poor times" pudding.

The upside-down cake was another popular item for resourceful pioneers. Fruit could be foraged from wild plants and placed in a skillet. Covered with batter, this "cake" was baked over an open fire—no oven required! It might seem an unusual dessert to our tastes, but give it a try on your next camping trip.

This advice, which appears in the 1877 edition of *Tried, Tested, Proved: The Home Cook Book*, Compiled by Ladies of Toronto and Chief Cities and Towns in Canada, is still sound today:

> In making cake, it is very desirable that the materials be of the finest quality. Sweet, fresh butter, eggs and good flour are the first essentials.
>
> The process of putting together is also quite an important feature, and where other methods are not given in this work by contributors, it would be well for the young housekeeper to observe the following directions: Never allow the butter to oil, but soften it by putting it in a moderately warm place before you commence other preparations for your cake; then put it into an earthen dish (tin, if not new, will discolour your cake as you stir it), and add your sugar; beat the butter and sugar to a cream; add the yolks of the eggs, then the milk, and lastly the beaten whites of the eggs and flour. Spices and liquors may be added after the yolks of the eggs are put in, and fruit should be put in with the flour.
>
> The oven should be pretty hot for small cakes, and moderate for larger.
>
> To ascertain if a large cake is sufficiently baked, pierce it with a broom-straw through the centre; if done the straw will come out free from dough; if not done, dough will adhere to the straw. Take it out of the tin about fifteen minutes after it is taken from the oven (not sooner), and do not turn it over on the top to cool.

Sandra Cranston-Corradini of The Cranston-Corradini School of Cooking has this to say about cake baking in Ontario:

> Cakes have changed in texture and consistency in the past 150 years. Ontario cakes were originally denser, spicier and greatly influenced by the cakes of the United Kingdom. They were entirely different from the distinctly French cakes or European cakes. Plain cakes were often made with drippings, rich cakes included fruit or nuts, and gingerbread was prepared in a multitude of ways. The recipes for fruitcake in

the 1800s far surpass any modern recipes that I have tried and for this reason I still use a family recipe from the late 1800s. I have found that the substitution of maple syrup for some of the sugar the recipe originally called for adds a distinctly Canadian touch.

The predilection for fruit continued for the next hundred years at which time luncheon or birthday cakes continued to include currants, sultanas, glacé cherries, dates, raisins and citrus. Modern cakes are generally lighter, and thankfully we are no longer required to know the average weight of a hen, duck or goose egg to make adjustments in recipes.

Carol Ferguson, co-author with Margaret Fraser of *A Century of Home Cooking: 1900 through the 90s*, explained to me that cake baking in Canada often directly parallels immigration, and is profoundly influenced by advances in technology and the prevailing fashion. Although Victorian recipes from England dominated early cookbooks, these influences were usually filtered via the United States. Even the British cookbooks used in Canadian homes were usually in editions republished in New York and Philadelphia.

In the first decade of the twentieth century, Edwardian fashion comprised elaborate meals and picnics, box socials, afternoon tea and elaborate banquets. In farmland, meals satisfied hearty appetites. Canadian wheat was already considered the best in the world. Cakes reflected the cultural heritage of the baker but made use of regional fruits and preserves. British influences dominated the early cookbooks, but Scandinavian, German, Icelandic and Scottish traditions were also maintained by home bakers.

By the 1920s cookbooks produced by the flour companies were common in home kitchens, baking ingredients were cheap and plentiful and home stoves offered relatively even baking temperatures. A glance through a Five Roses Flour cookbook of the era reveals familiar cake names among the 160 recipes: angel food, banana cake, black cake, seven fruit cakes, three molasses cakes, five layer cakes and, of course, the immensely popular jelly roll. Royal names for cakes, such as Prince Albert cake and King Edward cake, were popular at the time.

Toward the end of the 1930s, the Depression eased, and the home cook luxuriated in new technology that offered better ovens and refrigerators, as well as a more bountiful supply of fruits transported in new refrigerated boxcars. The Second World War had a significant influence on 1940s baking. While little changed in rural communities, urban bakers again had to contend with rationing of sugar and butter. Women marched off to work in the factories, and time spent in the kitchen began to shorten. The 1950s were a decade of plenty and technological advances that resulted in the most dramatic change in baking habits of the century. Cake mixes and one-bowl cake methods were made possible by the creation of emulsified shortening. This was the time of wacky cake and tomato soup cake. War brides from places other than the United Kingdom introduced more non-British flavors and techniques into the kitchen. Bakers still made traditional cakes and layer cakes, but mostly on special occasions.

In the 1960s, we begin to see the lost generations of bakers. My grandmother baked only one-bowl cakes, and my mother relied on cake mixes for birthday cakes. My family history doesn't include time spent together creaming butter and icing cakes, although the special occasions when we did bake are seared in my memory. Like many modern bakers, baking came to me later in life. The choice to become a chef and the subsequent training I undertook had much more influence on my baking skills than anything I learned at Grandma's knee.

Still, Canadians were baking. Cheesecakes, coffee cakes and pudding cakes were popular in the 1960s, as were snacking cakes and simple one-bowl cakes. In the 1970s, foods from around the globe became more popular, although most Canadians were still pretty conservative. Health food fads were common, and many people "turned off" white flour and sugar. Cakes were made with whole wheat flour, and carrots, zucchini, and other vegetables were added to loaves.

The 1980s and 1990s saw an explosion in food knowledge that continues today. People are hungry for beautiful food, and decadence, elegant simplicity and heritage baking are equally appreciated. Cakes can be rich and elaborate, resplendent with chocolate and nuts or very plain. At the restaurants where I have worked, the best-selling cakes have been either the richest chocolate or the simplest lemon poppy seed pound cake. We love top-quality ingredients: Belgian chocolate, Tahitian vanilla beans, macadamia nuts, fresh regional fruits and locally produced products such as maple syrup. We still favor butter cakes and sponge, but French cakes also suit our fancy, with layers of dacquoise, genoise and crunchy meringue. There is currently a tremendous fascination for the home arts, for baking cakes and pies and breads. We are embracing the hearth and our culinary history in a wonderful way and finding great solace and satisfaction there. My children are learning to bake at my knee; they will always remember little fingers dipped in flour and chocolate. My four-year-old son recently advised me when I wondered aloud if the cake in the oven was done, "Mom, you have to stick in a tester and see if it comes out clean." I looked at him in amazement. For him, the lexicon of the baker is already part of his speech. What marvelous cakes will he bake in years to come?

The Science behind Cake

When something is simple, we say it's "a piece of cake." However, I can only think that this expression refers to eating cake, because baking is really not simple at all. Of course, it's not rocket science, but baking a cake involves following a set of rules. To clarify these rules, I went to the experts, whose work or passion is developing the best recipes for cake. This chapter is the result of those conversations. I spoke with Regan Daley, pastry chef and author of one of the best reference works for the pastry kitchen, *In the Sweet Kitchen;* Daphna Rabinovich from *Canadian Living Magazine* and one of the popular personalities from Canadian Living Television; and Dufflet Rosenberg of Dufflet's Bakery in Toronto, known for its tantalizing creations.

In *Great Canadian Pies* I confessed that for years I was afflicted with the "Baking Curse." Nothing—nothing!—I baked turned out well. And I followed recipes to the letter—or so I thought. I am a natural-born cook, most alive in the kitchen where I can be consumed by my art. Adding a dash of this and a splash of that, I am inspired to concoct dishes. But baking relies on chemical reactions to work. An extra quarter cup of flour, the omission of a tablespoon of butter or baking on the wrong rack of the oven will all affect the end product. Bakers need to work like scientists. There are important rules to learn—and I learned every one of them the hard way. In this chapter, I clarify the science behind the cake so that you can, in fact, have your cake and eat it too. (I never did see the point of having cake if you weren't going to eat it.) Cakes can be separated into two major categories: butter cakes and foam (sponge, angel, chiffon, genoise) cakes. There are also quick breads, snacking cakes and muffins.

Oven Temperature

The optimum temperature for baking most cakes is 350°F (180°C). The heat must be high enough to create steam within the batter and cause that steam and other gases in the batter to expand and rise quickly. An oven that is too hot causes cake to rise unevenly, burn or be over-cooked on the exterior before the interior cooks. The batter must set completely without drying out. Too low a temperature and the cake will not rise sufficiently and may dry out before baking completely. Home ovens can vary in temperature by 50°F (10°C) or more; purchasing an inexpensive oven thermometer to confirm oven temperature before baking can be the best thing you ever do for your cakes. Rotate pans once cakes have finished two-thirds of their baking time to compensate for uneven oven temperature. Do not open the door before then, as the cake will not have gelatinized yet and the structure could be compromised. As Regan put it, "60 to 70% of cakes bake best at 350°F (180°C), but some bake better at 325°F (160°C) or 375°F (190°C). Things like cheesecakes want a nice slow bake at around 300°F (150°C) and a brownie or a fudge cake both benefit from a lower temperature."

Cake Pans

Aluminum pans are generally considered best for baking. Stainless steel causes uneven conduction, and dark or glass surfaces result in heat absorption. Avoid dark, nonstick pans, which allow the outside of the cake to overbake too quickly. "We use aluminum pans, but flexipans are good as well, particularly for mini cheesecakes," says Dufflet.

Fill pans one-half to two-thirds full. If the pan is too large, the cake will bake too quickly and be too thin with too much surface. If the pan is too small, the batter will overflow when it rises. Some bakers feel that butter cake layers baked in one pan then cut into layers are moister than layers baked in separate pans. Regan recommends filling butter cake pans "two-thirds to three-quarters full and sponge or angel food one-half to two-thirds. Again, the recipe is the best guide to follow."

Preparing the Pans

There are two options: the pans can be greased with shortening (butter has a higher water content and can burn or cause sticking) and dusted with flour, and the excess flour tapped out. Or the pans can be lined with parchment paper. My preference is parchment paper, since flouring results in a slight crust and will leave a light coloring on darker cakes. Pans should be prepared before the batter is mixed because cakes must be baked as soon as they are mixed so that air pockets do not deflate. Again, Regan recommends following the recipe:

> If the recipe is reliable, then do what they suggest. It's best not to make changes because you can run into trouble. Most often, I use butter with no trouble when I am flouring as well. If I grease only, I use shortening or vegetable oil cooking spray. Spraying nonstick pans can leave a gummy residue on the pan. Whatever you do, do it thoroughly—make sure you have a good coating of fat and a good coating of flour.

Placing cake pans on a baking sheet helps to conduct heat and will result in a better cake.

Measuring Techniques

Measuring techniques are an important part of successful baking and something that many novice bakers don't take seriously enough. In order for all the necessary chemical reactions to take place in the cake, the ingredients need to be present in exactly the right proportions. Proper measuring techniques are the only way to ensure that quantities are correct.

Professional pastry chefs weigh their ingredients for accuracy and that is really the best method. However, weighing hasn't caught on in home kitchens and most recipes reflect that. When measuring in volume, measure liquid in a liquid measuring cup. Glass is best; fill to the mark and check at eye level. Measure dry ingredients with dry measures that have flat tops for leveling. Spoon flour into the dry measure until it overflows, then level with a knife. Do not tap.

Ingredient Temperature

Almost all cake recipes will call for ingredients to be at room temperature. Butter, liquids in the cake and egg must emulsify (fully combine), and this won't happen if some ingredients are cold. The mixture may curdle or break, and the batter won't aerate. Butter should be just soft enough to leave an indentation when poked with your finger; butter that is too soft will not trap air and will collapse when beaten. Butter that is too cold is brittle. Regan says, "Eggs and milk will change the consistency of the butter; if they are cold, they will cause the butter to clump. Eggs need to be at their most elastic, and if they're too cold they will not increase in volume."

Baking Position

Bake cakes in the middle of the oven. That is where the temperature is most likely to be even and where there is room for air flow around the cake. The bottom of the oven is too hot and the top is too cool.

Protein

Flour, milk and eggs all add protein to the cake, which is necessary for its structure. Too little protein and the cake will collapse; too much and the cake will be tough and coarse-textured.

Tenderizers

Sugars, fats and egg yolks all shorten gluten strands (the protein in flour), which results in a tender, soft cake.

Liquid

Water, milk, juice and eggs add moisture, dissolve dry ingredients, disperse fat and flour, assist in the formation of carbon dioxide, provide steam for leavening and hydrate the protein and starch in the flour. This hydration results in gluten formation and is necessary for starch gelatinization, both of which are important to the cake's structure. Milk is the liquid of choice for most butter cakes, but water is best when using cocoa. Regan says,

> Liquid lubricates the batter and extends it. It adds moisture, which creates a broader structure so everything is not dense and tight. You get an airier product. If using milk, use 2% or homogenized for the fat and flavor.

Leaveners

Leaveners create gases in batter that work alongside steam to expand when the batter is heated. Eggs are natural leaveners because air is trapped in beaten eggs. Air is also trapped when fat and sugar are creamed together. Chemical leaveners—baking soda and baking powder—work by creating carbon dioxide, which expands air bubbles within fat cells. Unlike baking powder, which contains its own acid, baking soda requires another acid—such as sour cream, buttermilk, chocolate or fruit—to work. Too much chemical leavener will result in a fallen, crumbly cake, while too little will yield a small, dense cake. Chemical and natural leaveners work quickly, meaning that cakes must go into the oven immediately after mixing. Regan says,

> Leaveners' function is to release carbon dioxide. The difference between the chemical leaveners is that baking soda is instant; as soon as you combine it with an acid, it bubbles. Get the batter in the oven immediately because it's working *now*—it's instant. Baking powder is heat-sensitive and double acting; part of it works on contact, and part of it is activated by heat, so it's more reliable. Baking soda also needs an acid in the batter. Use baking soda with regular cocoa, but not with dutched cocoa, or your cake will not rise well because the acid in the dutched cocoa has already been neutralized.

How Cakes Rise

In the oven, cake batter expands due to steam and carbon dioxide trapped in air bubbles created and enveloped in fat during the mixing process; then the cell walls surrounding the air pockets rupture. At the same time, the starch in the batter gelatinizes and the egg proteins coagulate so the cake holds its shape. Timing is critical and is dictated by the oven temperature. Regan explains that

> Cakes rise through mechanical or chemical leavening; sometimes there are both in one cake. Mechanical leavening works with air; you trap air in the batter in either the fat or the eggs. In the heat of the oven, the air turns to steam, rises, inflates bubbles, evaporates and the bubbles break, but the area the bubbles occupied is empty because the structure of the cake (supplied by egg protein coagulation and starch gelatinization) is in place. This is why temperature is so important—too low a temperature and the sequence will not occur in the right order. Chemical leavening works the same way except the original genesis of the bubbles is a chemical reaction occurring in the batter.

Flour

In Canada we have excellent all-purpose flour, which will work best for most cakes. Recipes from other countries will call for cake and pastry flour because their all-purpose flour resembles our bread flour.

Regan says,

> I usually use all-purpose flour or a combination of all-purpose and pastry flour. Canadian all-purpose flour is very high quality with a relatively low gluten content at 9% to 11% while our cake and pastry flour is 7% to 8% protein. Follow the recipe; don't play around with substituting flours if you're not sure. The flour has to have enough strength and structure to support the cake plus additional ingredients like fruit, maple syrup, sour cream and chocolate. All are heavy in a batter and need a strong flour to support them. I find a combination offers the tenderness of cake and pastry flour with the structure of all-purpose flour.

Daphna says,

> About 3% of the baking I do is with cake and pastry flour. Canadian all-purpose flour will make you the best muffins, cookies, cakes and bread. I do use cake and pastry flour for ladyfingers and fine things like that.

Eggs

Eggs provide structure to the cake by trapping air and holding moisture. Regan notes that

> Eggs aid in leavening by being good emulsifiers; they entrap and hold air. Egg whites leaven differently than whole eggs, they literally trap air themselves. Eggs coagulate at a relatively low temperature and provide structure to the cake until the starches in the flour gelatinize. They also moisten the cake due to their ability to retain moisture, and this is maximized on coagulation.

Butter

Butter provides flavor, traps air and coats the protein in the flour to reduce gluten formation. Regan agrees that

> There is no replacement for butter; it is essential to cake. Butter imparts flavor, tenderness and moisture. Butter acts in partnership with sugar as a mechanical leavener, because the fat molecules hold in the air that is incorporated due to friction with the sugar. The result is this natural aeration, and then when the steam gets involved, the bubbles expand.

Shortening

Shortening is often used in commercial baking because it will aerate at a wider range of temperatures than butter. This makes it more foolproof, but at the same time shortening is less flavorful than butter. Emulsified shortenings made possible the one-bowl method of mixing, which has been very popular with busy bakers since the 1950s. Regan says,

> In my experience you can have the best of both worlds by using a combination of butter and shortening. You get the flavor of butter and the behavior of shortening. The texture is more velvety, and the mouth feel can be beautiful.

Sugar

Sugar's sharp edges hold air in fat. Sugar is also hydroscopic, meaning it absorbs liquid and aids in providing structure to the cake. Regan cautions,

> Do not use superfine sugar for creaming because you want the big grains of granulated sugar. Think of rocks under a blanket; boulders are too big, but sand is too small and will hold no air. Rocks are just the right size to keep the blanket up and hold in lots of air. The only real situation where I would recommend superfine sugar is for angel food cake where you want the sugar to dissolve as fast as possible—otherwise you want nothing finer than a granulated sugar.

Mixing Methods

Mixing the batter works to combine ingredients, incorporate air cells and develop texture. It is best done with a good quality stand-up mixer, a handheld mixer or, bless your strong arms, a whisk.

Creaming

The creaming method incorporates air cells into fat and is best for butter cakes. These cakes also need a chemical leavener for aeration. When creaming fat, work at low speeds to prevent raising the temperature of the fat, resulting in the loss of air cells. Regan agrees, saying,

> Creaming is a mechanical process blending butter and sugar. It's really more than mixing; it distributes sugar crystals evenly throughout the fat, and in doing so incorporates as much air into the mixture as possible. If all you wanted to do was blend them, then you would just melt them together, but you want the butter to be as light and big and airy as possible. It is very hard to overmix at this stage, you're further ahead mixing more than less. Make sure to scrape down so you're not creaming the same half over and over again. If using a mechanical mixer, use the medium to high setting. After adding eggs to creamed butter and sugar, incorporate remaining ingredients at low speed or by hand to avoid overmixing.

Whipping

Whipping is best for genoise, which relies on air whipped into eggs for leavening. Whip eggs and sugar over warm water until very light and tripled in volume. Quickly but gently fold in sifted flour and then oil or melted butter. Regan says,

> The trick is this, when whisking you want to make a giant vertical circle; impregnate the mixture with as much air as possible. Fold air in, reach in and lift the whisk up and whoop in as much air as possible, don't just mix at the bottom of the bowl but also vertically. That's the goal with sponge cakes. Eggs are your leavener, so you want to use the whisk not just to blend but to entrap air. Same goes for any time that you want to whip egg whites as well. Use as big a balloon whisk as possible with as many wires as you can find, the finer the better.

Sponge cakes are leavened with air whipped into eggs, but chemical leaveners may be added. The batter is assembled with beaten yolks and other ingredients, then the egg whites are whipped to firm peaks with sugar and folded into the batter. When finished, these cakes are often soaked in liqueur or syrup or layered with moist flavorful ingredients such as custard or chocolate.

Angel food cakes are leavened solely with whipped egg whites. The batter is turned into an ungreased tube pan, and while it bakes, the batter climbs the sides of the pan and is held there. Fat is anathema to these cakes, which must cool inverted in the pan as the only thing that keeps them from collapsing is gravity.

Chiffon cakes are leavened with whipped egg whites but also employ chemical leaveners. This allows for the addition of egg yolk and vegetable oil, making a moister and richer cake than angel food. The batter is baked in an ungreased tube pan and climbs the sides of the pan.

Unmolding Cakes

Regan comments,

> Unless it's a brownie, a flourless chocolate cake or something sloppy, wait 5 to 10 minutes to let the cake cool on a rack, then run a knife around it and invert onto a wire rack. Most cakes benefit from cooling before you eat them. It's a good idea to ice the cake so it stays moist. Sheet cakes can be inverted onto a wire rack, then the parchment paper peeled off. If making a roll cake, leave it on parchment until semi-cool, and that side will be extra tender due to steaming.

Storing Cakes

Once baked, most cakes will do best at room temperature. The cool temperature of the refrigerator hardens most baked goods and should be avoided. However, some cream-style and custard cakes need to be stored in the refrigerator; follow the instructions in the recipe. Many types of cakes will freeze very well for up to four months. Wrap in plastic and then foil before freezing. To defrost, bring the cake to room temperature without disturbing the wrapping. It pays to have extra icing on hand in case frozen cakes need a little touch-up.

Iced cakes should be defrosted overnight in the refrigerator to prevent excessive moisture formation.

Dufflet had this advice for the home baker: "Find your favorite recipe and perfect it, then this will be the cake you can bake with very little stress."

Daphna's Baking Tips

There is a cake for every season, for every occasion. I'm a big believer in eating dessert; I make cakes for all occasions. Life's short; eat cake, have a good time making it and a better time eating it.

As your confidence grows, so will your comfort zone and your skill. Just keep on baking; every experienced baker has had failures, but the more you bake the better you will be at it. You don't have a lot of freedom in baking; it's very scientific. Having said that, once you've made a cake often enough and you have a certain level of confidence, your individual artistry and freedom can come in.

Here are some tips:

1. Take your time.

2. Make sure all your ingredients are at room temperature. Room temperature is between 68°F (20°C) and 72°F (22°C).

3. Know how to measure; spoon and sweep.

4. Pay attention to pan sizes.

5. Buy a heavy aluminum cake pan and, if you can, invest in a good stand-up mixer and some graduated bowls—something that you can mix two eggs in all the way up to the largest bowl available.

6. Try a fine sugar for meringues; it dissolves better.

7. I am so persnickety about butter; I will never have salted butter in my kitchen.

8. Always use good-quality cocoa for chocolate cakes.

9. When creaming, beat the butter first, to get it going. There are lots of shortcuts in recipes, but taking that extra step can really help your cakes.

10. Experiment with different brands of flour and find one you're comfortable with. The same goes for butter.

11. You can't feel cakes the same way you can feel pastry so an advantage is taken away from you, but eventually you will develop an instinct for the look of the batter.

12. You can't rush a cake.

13. Get to know the temperature of your oven; you have to have an oven thermometer. After the first 30 minutes in the oven, the structure of the cake is set; if your oven is hotter in the back, rotate the cake.

14. Check your cake at the earliest time on the recipe to see if it's baked.

15. A good baker can tell by smell when the cake is done.

An Eye for Detail: Cake Decorating

Cake takes many forms. The simple, unadorned pound cake with a light dusting of icing sugar answers a hunger for comfort and simple pleasure. However, a child's blue-monster birthday cake and an elegant three-tiered wedding cake celebrate life's milestones. Each requires a practiced hand, a genuine effort and a modicum of talent. Some cakes are best with a dollop of whipped cream and a few fresh berries; others require rolled fondant, gum paste sculpture and a steady hand with a paintbrush. At the very least, we always want our cakes to be pretty.

This chapter is dedicated to the art of making a cake lovely. Fillings, frostings, techniques, equipment and all manner of edible adornment are discussed here. Much of this information was derived through conversations with Monika Paradi, who has been decorating cakes in Toronto for 20 years. Monika trained at McCall's School of Cake Decorating and is past president of The Canadian Society of Sugar Artistry, and a member of The International Cake Exploration Society.

Equipment

Basic Equipment

These are things you can't live without.

Baking sheet: Placing a filled cake pan on a baking sheet will result in more even baking and a better cake. Thick aluminum sheets are better than dark, nonstick sheets.

Cake comb: This is an essential tool; it will help even the absolute novice to spread an even coating of icing.

Cake pans: You will need a few different-sized pans, because the wrong size pan can result in failure. A 9-inch (1.5 L) round pan is essential, as are an 8-inch (2 L) or 9-inch (2.5 L) square pan, a 9- x 5-inch (2 L) loaf pan, a 10-inch (2.5 L) bundt pan and a muffin pan for large muffins. Buy heavy aluminum pans; dark, nonstick surfaces bake too quickly and cause overbrowning and peaking. Even glass pans are preferable to nonstick or coated pans; the new rubber flexipans work very well—they are particularly effective for releasing the cake and are easy to clean.

Cooling rack: Placing a hot cake on the rack allows air to circulate for even cooling.

Dry measuring cups: A set that gives the measures in imperial and metric is most helpful. Each cup measures right to the top so dry ingredients can be leveled off.

Handheld mixer: For beating almost everything.

Liquid measuring cup: Liquid must be measured in a glass cup measure. Pour liquid into the cup and bend down to read the measure at eye level.

Measuring spoons: A set that gives measures in imperial and metric is most helpful. Each spoon measures right to the top so dry ingredients can be leveled off.

Mixing bowls: A set of stainless steel bowls will last a lifetime. They're lightweight, easy to store and perfect for everything from whipping egg whites to mixing batter.

Oven thermometer: An absolute must! Always check the temperature of your oven before baking the cake. Ovens can vary in temperature by 50°F (10°C), which can have a tremendous effect on your cake.

Palette knife/offset palette: For spreading icing.

Parchment paper: For lining cake pans and eliminating the cake-sticking-to-the-pan problem once and for all.

Rubber spatula: Great for mixing, spreading and scooping every last bit of batter out of a bowl.

Ruler: For measuring cake layers.

Saucepan: For making glazes, custards, coulis and sauces.

Sifter: For sifting dry ingredients.

Wire whisk: Almost every recipe will require some whisking of ingredients; the loops of wire do the best job of mixing ingredients. A balloon whisk is handy for whipping air into cream or egg whites.

Wooden spoon: Great for mixing, creaming, folding and stirring. It won't react with cookware and gets into corners and along the curve of bowls.

Equipment for the More Advanced Cake Baker

Cake server: For serving the cake.

Cake stand: Buy one that rotates so you can easily spread frosting or decorate the sides of the cake.

Cake tester: Toothpicks work, but a metal tester can be reused.

Candy thermometer: I use a visual test for cooked sugar and caramel, but a thermometer ensures accuracy.

Cardboard rounds: For placing under cake so it can be easily moved or stacked (for tiered cakes).

Chocolate thermometer: Necessary if tempering chocolate.

Citrus zester: Easily removes zest, leaving pith behind.

Coffee grinder: For grinding spices and nuts.

Copper bowls and pots: Copper bowls are lovely for whipping egg whites, and copper pots transmit heat evenly.

Food processor: Very helpful for chopping, pureeing and some mixing tasks.

Immersion blender: Great for blending ingredients in the bowl or pan.

Insulating cake strips: For insulating the sides of the cake pan so the cake doesn't peak.

Kitchen scale: Most professional pastry chefs and bakers weigh their ingredients for absolute accuracy.

Nutmeg grater: Nothing beats freshly ground nutmeg.

Other cake pans: Collecting cake pans can become an obsession. Buy whatever suits your fancy— mini pans, springform pans, brioche pans, molds, rings and character pans for children's cakes.

Pastry brush: For brushing liquid onto cake.

Piping bag with several decorating tips and a coupler: For piping borders, decorations and words on cake. The coupler allows you to change tips without emptying the bag.

Pizza wheel: Handy for cutting rolled fondant.

Plastic and glass cake dome: For storing, displaying and transporting cakes.

Reusable nonstick sheet: Works as well as or better than parchment and can be reused.

Rolling pin: For rolling marzipan or fondant.

Serrated knife: For cutting cakes.

Stand-up mixer: A very sexy piece of equipment. A heavy-duty, good-quality mixer should last your family for more than one generation.

Equipment for the Serious Decorator

Cake drums: For holding heavy cakes.

Cake leveler: Important only if you're making something like a wedding cake and you want perfectly even levels.

Crimping tools: For making patterns in rolled fondant.

Dowels: To support tiers of wedding cakes.

Dredger: For dusting cakes with powders.

Gum paste cutters and cookie cutters: For making flowers and shapes.

Paintbrushes: For painting color onto fondant, marzipan or gum paste, for smoothing out lines and for getting into small spaces.

Plastic squeeze bottles: For applying sugar syrup.

Stamps: For embossing fondant; the pattern can then be painted.

Textured rolling pin: For making designs in fondant.

Trowel: Good for spreading an even layer of icing over a large surface.

Icings and Fillings

Choosing the best icing and filling to accent and decorate a cake is critical. Ideally, the flavor, intensity and character of the icing should complement the taste and texture of the cake. The amount of frosting used will also vary; for example, you will use less of a very rich dense chocolate icing, but may want to slather on whipped cream. Sometimes an icing is chosen solely for its decorative value and ability; royal icing, for example, is intensely sweet, but its eye appeal keeps decorators coming back for more.

Royal Icing

Royal icing is made of icing sugar, egg whites, lemon juice and coloring (optional). With practice, you can learn to pipe all manner of designs, flowers and shapes for cake decorating. Decorations can be made days ahead and will become hard as plaster, but may tend to crumble. As for taste, royal icing is very sweet and nothing more. See recipe on page 2.

Rolled Fondant and Sugar Paste Icing

Rolled fondant can be made or purchased as white, ivory or chocolate by the pound in tubs at bakers' supply stores. Rolled fondant is frequently used on wedding cakes. Rolled and draped over the finished cake, fondant makes a stunning and smooth finish. It can also be used for cutouts, or combined with a little water to make a piping consistency for borders and accents. Flower cutouts are popular for wedding cakes and teddy bears are always a hit with children.

Fondant can be touched without leaving marks, and it colors beautifully with paste food coloring. Paint designs and accents using a mixture of alcohol and paste color, or use liquid food coloring to airbrush the surface.

There is a new type of rolled icing made of marshmallow cream and icing sugar kneaded together until the consistency is right for modeling or rolling. Unfortunately, this type of rolled icing doesn't dry as well as traditional fondant. See recipe on page 139.

Poured Fondant

Poured fondant is used mainly for petit fours, and is very sticky even when dry.

Buttercream

Buttercream is the most popular icing with home bakers and decorators. It is made by slowly beating a sugar syrup into egg yolks, then beating in butter. It's rich and sweet and can be used to fill, frost and pipe. Decorations of buttercream can be piped the day before and then refrigerated. Often a wedding cake is covered with fondant then decorated with buttercream.

If buttercream is too cold, it will be firm and difficult to spread; too warm and it will run over the cake. When making special occasion cakes, make extra buttercream to reserve for touchups. See recipe on page 3.

European Buttercream

This is also known as Italian meringue and is Monika's favorite because it is very smooth and doesn't crust over. To prepare European buttercream, beat egg whites until stiff, and whip in a hot sugar syrup until cool. Then add butter for a smooth finish. See recipe on page 4.

Chocolate and Ganache

Chocolate and ganache are perennial favorites. Why? Well, because they're chocolate, of course. Chocolate coatings and fillings can be mousses, buttercream or even pure melted chocolate. Ganache is made by melting bittersweet or semisweet chocolate in hot cream. Ganache can also be flavored, or cooled and whipped for a light ganache filling. It is also ideal for making truffles and for icing cakes. See recipes on page 18.

Curl or shave chocolate for a quick, easy garnish. To make curls, buy a large (the larger the better) milk or white chocolate bar. These are high in cocoa butter and curl well. Warm the bar between your hands, then shave off the curls with a warmed, sharp potato peeler or French knife. Chocolate curls can also be made by gently warming chocolate and pouring it onto a marble slab or the back of a stainless steel baking sheet; when the chocolate sets, scrape the curls up with a palette knife.

Use melted chocolate to drizzle designs over a frosted cake.

Temper chocolate couverture and pour it into molds or use it to make chocolate leaves. The room should be neither too warm nor too cold (65°F to 70°F/18°C to 21°C), and wearing plastic gloves ensures that the warmth of your hands doesn't affect the chocolate.

For leaves, brush the melted chocolate over the underside of several real leaves and place on parchment paper on a plate or tray, then refrigerate to harden. Peel leaves away from hardened chocolate. (This also works with melted white chocolate.)

Chocolate plastic is made from chocolate and corn syrup, and can be rolled or molded. Monika says, "I use chocolate plastic for roses. Reusing is dicey, so I make a batch and use it all right away. While using, I keep it in my pocket to maintain a nice pliable temperature." As with gum paste, it is best to work with a nonstick rolling pin and board.

Marzipan

Marzipan is a sweetened almond paste that can be rolled to cover cakes or molded into decorative pieces. Many cake decorators tend to use chocolate plastic, gum paste or fondant because, while marzipan has a superior taste, it is expensive, has a tendency to be greasy, won't dry overnight and is not really smooth. Although many traditional cakes, such as fruitcakes, were covered in marzipan first, then royal icing, this method is out of fashion now. Marzipan makes a great barrier between a strawberry or other fruit filling and fondant, keeping the fondant from staining.

Gum Paste

Gum paste is made of egg white, sugars, gelatin, gum tragacanth and shortening, then cured for 24 hours and cut into pieces. The pieces can be colored and rolled very thin, using small nonstick plastic rollers and boards. Gum paste works well for elaborate decorations because it dries very hard. Bakers' supply shops sell cutting and modeling tools for gum paste.

Food Coloring

Food coloring comes in liquid, paste and dust. Color foods the day before you plan to use them because the color will intensify overnight. Higher fat products don't take color well; buttercreams are the most difficult to tint a deep color.

Caramel

Caramel is made by melting sugar until the sugar begins to brown (caramelize). This hot golden syrup can be poured into molds, drizzled into freeform designs, used to make cages or poured into sheets and broken into shards for decoration. See recipe on page 16.

Meringue

Use meringue to make nests, pavlovas or meringue layers. Sandwich layers with buttercream, genoise, mousse or any type of layer that suits. For interesting seasonal cookies or holiday decorations, pipe meringue into star shapes, bake to dry and sprinkle with edible glitter.

Flowers and Leaves

Fresh, edible flowers are always beautiful. Washed fresh flowers can be placed directly on the cake or, if you can be sure that your edible flowers have not been sprayed with pesticides, sugar them by brushing on egg white then sprinkling with very fine sugar. Fresh greenery is also popular, but use the same caution to ensure that greenery is edible and has not been sprayed with pesticides. Keep flowers and greenery in separate containers and set on the cake at the last minute. Ensure that there are no drops of moisture on the flowers, which will mar the fondant or icing. With flowers, as with all decorations, it pays to have a few extra on hand in case you need to hide an imperfection in the design.

Dessert Sauces

Pastry chefs in restaurants are more likely to decorate a single serving of cake on the plate rather than the whole cake. Even elaborately decorated cakes can benefit from some extra work on the plate. Custards, coulis, ganache, syrup or caramel can be drizzled over a piece of cake or onto the plate. Try creating a two-tone effect by using two sauces together, like custard and berry coulis, or chocolate and fruit syrup.

Putting It All Together

This is where patience and an eye for detail are important. First allow the cake to cool, then place it on your turntable. Have a look at it. Is it even? If not, use a long serrated knife to cut away peaks or tall edges. If you are cutting the cake in half horizontally, use a ruler to determine where to cut notches into all sides of the cake at an even height. Cut into the cake 1/2 inch (1 cm) while turning it. Keep the knife aligned with the notches to ensure the cut is even. Go around once more, cutting 1 inch (2.5 cm) further into the cake. Use a length of dental floss pulled through the cake to cut the center. Slide a cake board (or thin cardboard disc) under the top layer and remove it.

Sponge cakes may be brushed with liqueur or syrup at this time. If filling the cake, spread a layer of filling 1/8-inch (0.25 cm) to 1/4-inch (0.5 cm) thick. Rich, dense fillings, such as chocolate, should be used more sparingly than lighter varieties, like whipped cream. This process of creating different layers is called torting the cake.

Place the second layer over the filling and align it with the bottom layer. Repeat with remaining layers, as necessary.

To Frost the Cake

Most frostings need a "crumb coat," which seals any remaining crumbs into the cake so they won't appear in the finished frosting. Simply brush loose crumbs from the cake, then use an offset spatula to spread a thin layer of frosting over the top and sides of the cake to seal in loose crumbs. Any indentations in the cake can be filled with icing at this time. Keep this frosting separate from the large batch; you do not want crumbs in the final coat. Refrigerate cake for 5 minutes before applying the final coat. For the final coat, smooth frosting over the top, then the sides of the cake. Swirl or spike the surface as you like; a perfectly even, smooth finish is difficult to attain, and novice cake decorators are advised to use a technique that better hides small errors. Use a cake comb to create a textured design on the top or sides of the cake.

Once the cake is frosted, the icing or a complementary topping can be piped on top; roses, script, beads, stars and borders are just a few of the options. Alternatively, patterns can be dusted on set frosting, using icing sugar or cocoa and a stencil.

As a final step, nuts, candies or coconut can be pressed into the sides of the cake.

Children's Cakes

Children love both brightly colored cakes and character cakes. Purchase a mold of a favorite cartoon character, then use colored buttercream for details. For numbers, bake a slab cake (a long, rectangular cake) then make a paper pattern for the desired number. Fill the cake, then cut it out, using the template. Buttercream is the best bet for decorating children's cakes because it pipes well and, usually, little gourmets like the taste. My experience is that vanilla cakes are the favorite of the tot set.

Wedding Cakes

Traditional fruitcake has been waning in popularity over the past few decades. Today, anything goes—except when baking for a large group; in that case, avoid using nuts in case of peanut allergies. Vanilla, chocolate, carrot and banana are now standard for wedding cakes. Most are made of three tiers supported by wooden dowels (or even large plastic straws) running through the cake. Layers are decorated separately, and each is placed on its own disc. Another disc may be placed in the center of the top cake to support a flower arrangement or other centerpiece, with a dowel situated directly underneath to support it.

The bottom layer of the cake is placed on a thick, solid, drum board, which will be sturdy enough to support the entire weight of the cake. Rolled fondant is an excellent choice for covering cake layers, and it can then be decorated as you please. When transporting the cake, move each layer separately and reassemble at the function. Remember to bring along extra decorating supplies for touch-ups.

How to Store a Decorated Cake

Store decorated cake layers in the refrigerator, loosely covered with plastic wrap. Remove from the refrigerator an hour before moving or serving the cake. During this hour, do not disturb the wrapping or condensation from the wrapping will end up on the cake. Remember that moisture will mar the surface you have worked hard to attain.

The Cake Commandments

Follow these simple rules to help you bake great Canadian cakes.

Have fun.

•

Practice and experiment.

•

The temperature of ingredients is vital. For most cakes, ingredients must be at room temperature. Butter must be soft enough so an indented finger leaves a mark; not softer, not harder.

•

Always preheat the oven. Use an oven thermometer to make sure the temperature is correct. Many ovens run hot or cold.

•

Measure ingredients properly. Do not estimate. Buy dry and liquid measures; use the scoop-and-level method of measuring dry ingredients and check liquid ingredients at eye level.

Unless otherwise directed, use all-purpose flour and unsalted butter.

•

Begin by creaming butter, then whip in granulated sugar until it's very light
and fluffy. You really can't overmix at this stage.

•

When the time comes to add the flour mixture, mix slowly or change to a wooden
spoon or rubber spatula. Overmixing at this stage will result in a tough cake.

•

When whipping egg whites, make sure all utensils are squeaky clean.

•

Use the pan size specified in the recipe.

•

Use heavy aluminum pans and prepare as instructed in the recipe.
Fill one-third to two-thirds full for butter cakes and two-thirds to three-quarters
full for sponge.

•

As soon as all ingredients have been incorporated, put the cake in the
oven immediately.

•

Bake on the middle rack, unless the recipe specifies otherwise, and rotate the pan
after a half hour. Never open the oven before a half hour has passed.

•

Check the cake for doneness after the shortest time recommended.

•

Let cool for 5 to 10 minutes, then remove cake from pan.

•

Allow cake to cool completely before frosting or filling.

•

Choose a frosting or filling that best suits the taste and texture of the cake.

•

Again, have fun!

The Bare Necessities

Here are the icings, glazes and buttercreams you will need to make your cake a thing of beauty. Also included are structural components of some cakes: genoise, mousse and meringue. Try designing your own cake; mix and match cake layers with fillings and frostings as your fancy dictates. As you experiment, you will learn about complementary flavors, consistencies and textures. And, as I have said before, even your failures will likely be welcome. It is a cold heart indeed that would condemn you for using too many chocolate layers or for overdoing it with the buttercream.

One tip: balance is as good a thing in cake as in life. If the cake you've chosen is rich and dense, a lighter filling and frosting may be your best bet. Some flavors, like some people, were obviously made for each other. Chocolate and coffee. Maple and pecan. Almonds and honey. Many recipes in the book use the basic cake parts described here.

Royal Icing

With practice you can learn to pipe all manner of designs, flowers and shapes for cake decorating. Once dry, royal icing becomes hard, but it tends to crumble. This icing will not work in a humid environment.

1 1/2 cups (375 mL)	icing sugar
2	egg whites
1/4 tsp (1 mL)	cream of tartar
	food coloring (optional)

Rinse all bowls and utensils with vinegar, then hot water. Allow to air dry.

Beat 3/4 cup (175 mL) of the icing sugar with egg whites and cream of tartar until smooth. Add remaining 3/4 cup (175 mL) of icing sugar, and continue to beat until icing is glossy and stiff and holds peaks. If necessary, beat in additional sugar. If icing becomes too stiff, beat in drops of water until the consistency is right for piping.

Beat in food coloring until desired shade is obtained (color will intensify if left overnight). Cover icing with a damp towel until ready to use and while piping.

Makes about 1 cup (250 mL).

Buttercream

This basic frosting is used for many cakes in the book. Do not stir sugar syrup once the sugar has dissolved, and ensure the whipped egg yolks are cool before adding the butter. If the buttercream separates or curdles, beat vigorously and it should come together.

1 cup (250 mL)	granulated sugar
1/4 tsp (1 mL)	cream of tartar
6	egg yolks, room temperature
1 1/2 cups (375 mL)	unsalted butter, room temperature, cubed
2 tsp (10 mL)	pure vanilla extract

In a heavy-bottomed saucepan, dissolve sugar and cream of tartar in 1/2 cup (125 mL) water. Bring to a boil, uncovered, and boil until syrup dropped into a glass of water forms a soft ball (234°F/112°C).

Meanwhile, beat egg yolks in a stainless steel bowl over hot water until light and thick. Remove from heat and beat syrup into yolks in a thin, slow stream. Continue to beat until the yolks have cooled. Beat in butter, one cube at a time, fully incorporating each piece before the next addition. Stir in vanilla.

Use immediately or cover and refrigerate. To restore the texture of cold buttercream, let it warm to room temperature, then stir vigorously.

Makes 3 cups (750 mL).

European Buttercream

This differs from regular buttercream in that it is made with egg whites rather than yolks. Cake decorators like this frosting's satiny smooth finish. Choose a liqueur that complements the flavor of your cake.

4	egg whites, room temperature
1 cup (250 mL)	granulated sugar
1/4 tsp (1 mL)	cream of tartar
1 1/2 cups (375 mL)	unsalted butter, room temperature
1 tsp (5 mL)	pure vanilla extract
2 tbsp (25 mL)	crème de cacao (or preferred liqueur)

In a clean glass or stainless steel bowl, whip egg whites with sugar and cream of tartar. Place bowl in a wide pot with enough simmering water to immerse bowl to the level of the eggs. Beat whites until they are warmed, no more than 5 minutes. Remove from heat and whip until cool, thick and glossy.

Beat in butter, 1 tbsp (15 mL) at a time, fully incorporating each piece before the next addition. Slowly beat in vanilla and crème de cacao.

Use immediately or cover and refrigerate. To restore the texture of cold buttercream, let it warm to room temperature, then stir vigorously.

Makes 3 cups (750 mL).

Chocolate Buttercream

If you are, like me, a hopeless chocolate addict, see "Canada's Favorite: Chocolate Cake"
for some marvelously decadent creations or use this luscious
buttercream to create your own.

1/4 cup (50 mL)	whipping cream
1 2/3 cups (400 mL)	semisweet chocolate chips
2 tbsp (25 mL)	chocolate liqueur
2 tsp (10 mL)	pure vanilla extract
1 cup (250 mL)	granulated sugar
6	egg yolks, room temperature
1 1/2 cups (375 mL)	unsalted butter, room temperature

Warm whipping cream over low heat; add chocolate and stir until melted. Stir in liqueur and vanilla, then set aside to cool.

In a heavy-bottomed saucepan, dissolve sugar in 1/2 cup (125 mL) water. Bring to a boil, uncovered, and boil until syrup dropped into a glass of water forms a soft ball (234°F/112°C).

Meanwhile, beat egg yolks in a stainless steel bowl over hot water until light and thick. Remove from heat and beat syrup into yolks in a thin, slow stream. Continue to beat until the yolks have cooled.

Beat in butter, 1 tbsp (15 mL) at a time, fully incorporating each piece before the next addition. Vigorously stir in chocolate mixture, using a rubber spatula.

Use immediately or cover and refrigerate. To restore the texture of cold buttercream, let it warm to room temperature, then stir vigorously.

Makes 3 1/2 cups (875 mL).

Mocha Buttercream

Mellow mocha goes well with so many flavors. Use this buttercream as a filling or frosting for chocolate, fruit, custard or nut cakes.

2 oz (60 g)	bittersweet chocolate, chopped
2 tbsp (25 mL)	strong, brewed espresso
2 tbsp (25 mL)	coffee liqueur
2 tsp (10 mL)	pure vanilla extract
1 cup (250 mL)	granulated sugar
6	egg yolks, room temperature
1 1/2 cups (375 mL)	unsalted butter, room temperature

Stir chocolate in hot espresso until melted; stir in liqueur and vanilla, then set aside to cool.

In a heavy-bottomed saucepan, dissolve sugar in 1/2 cup (125 mL) water. Bring to a boil, uncovered, and boil until syrup dropped into a glass of water forms a soft ball (234°F/112°C).

Meanwhile, beat egg yolks in a stainless steel bowl over hot water until light and thick. Remove from heat, beat syrup into yolks in a thin, slow stream and continue to beat until the yolks have cooled.

Beat in butter, 1 tbsp (15 mL) at a time, fully incorporating each piece before the next addition. Vigorously stir in coffee mixture, using a rubber spatula.

Use immediately or cover and refrigerate. To restore the texture of cold buttercream, let it warm to room temperature, then stir vigorously.

Makes 3 cups (750 mL).

Basic Glaze

This glaze takes no time to prepare and adds a simple finishing touch to plain cakes.

2 tbsp (25 mL)	lemon juice
1 tbsp (15 mL) (approx.)	apple juice
1 1/2 cups (375 mL)	icing sugar, sifted
1/2	vanilla bean

Whisk juices into icing sugar, adjusting liquid as necessary to achieve a thick but pourable glaze. You may need up to 1 tbsp (15 mL) more apple juice. Slice vanilla bean down the center and scrape seeds out into glaze. Whisk until smooth.

Makes about 3/4 cup (175 mL).

Maple Glaze

Spring isn't complete without a visit to a sugar bush to watch maple syrup being made in an old-fashioned boiler. For days after, we serve everything with maple syrup on top.

1/2 cup (125 mL)	maple syrup
2 tbsp (25 mL)	unsalted butter, cold and cubed

Heat syrup in a small saucepan over medium-high heat, then whisk in cubes of butter. Use at room temperature.

Makes 1/2 cup (125 mL).

Cream Cheese Icing

Thick cream cheese icing is great with carrot cake (see recipe on page 63).

1 pound (500 g)	full fat cream cheese	5 cups (1.25 L)	icing sugar, sifted
1/2 cup (125 mL)	unsalted butter, room temperature	1 tbsp (15 mL)	pure vanilla extract
		2 tbsp (25 mL)	orange liqueur

Using a food processor, pulse cream cheese and butter until smooth. Pulse in icing sugar, 1 cup (250 mL) at a time.

Stir in vanilla and liqueur.

Use immediately or cover and refrigerate. To restore the texture of cold icing, let it warm to room temperature, then stir vigorously.

Makes about 4 cups (1 L).

Coulis

This sauce can be made with a variety of fresh fruits; choose the most vivid color for decorating cake plates.

1 package (10 oz/425 g)	frozen berries, thawed or	3 tbsp (50 mL) (approx.)	fruit sugar
2 cups (500 mL)	berries	1 tbsp (15 mL) (approx.)	liqueur or lemon juice

Using a food processor, process all the ingredients, then taste. Add sugar, liqueur or lemon juice to taste and to achieve a texture that coats the back of a spoon.

Use a rubber spatula to push the sauce through a fine sieve to remove any seeds or skins.

Refrigerate for up to 3 days.

Makes 1 1/2 cups (375 mL).

Rich Custard

This is my own rich custard recipe. Made without cornstarch or flour, it relies on egg yolk and cream for its consistency. It first appeared as a part of a trifle recipe in a Christmas feature I wrote for President's Choice® Magazine.

9	egg yolks
1/2 cup (125 mL)	granulated sugar
2 cups (500 mL)	whipping cream
1	vanilla bean, split or
1 tsp (5 mL)	pure vanilla extract

In a large bowl, beat yolks and sugar until a thick, pale ribbon falls from the beater when it is lifted.

Heat cream with vanilla bean (if using), in a heavy-bottomed pot over medium heat until just steaming. Whisking constantly, slowly add hot cream to egg mixture. Pour custard back into pot and return to low heat, stirring constantly, but gently, with a wooden spoon until mixture thickens slightly, about 10 minutes. Be careful not to scramble the eggs by applying too much heat or not stirring.

Remove from heat and continue stirring for 2 minutes. Remove vanilla bean or stir in pure vanilla extract (if using).

Pour through a fine strainer into a chilled bowl and set over ice water until cool. Cover with plastic wrap and refrigerate for up to 2 days.

Makes about 2 1/2 cups (625 mL).

Troy's Custard

Troy the Dessert Boy was our pastry chef at André's, and this was his custard. We served it in meringue rounds covered in chocolate and fresh berries, or between layers of moist cake.

1 3/4 cups (425 mL)	milk
3/4 cup (175 mL)	granulated sugar
1/4 cup (50 mL)	cornstarch
pinch	salt
1	egg +
1	yolk

Heat milk until hot.

Combine dry ingredients, then whisk in 1/4 cup (50 mL) of hot milk until smooth. Whisk in remaining milk, then egg and yolk.

Cook over a simmering double boiler, whisking constantly, until thick, about 5 minutes.

Pour through a fine strainer into a container, and set over ice water until cool. Cover with plastic wrap and refrigerate for up to 2 days.

Makes about 2 cups (500 mL).

Genoise

This is chef André's genoise. It is the only version of this cake I have encountered that uses cornstarch. Genoise is tender and delicious all on its own, but soaked in liqueur and filled with custard or buttercream—well, it takes the cake.

1 cup + 1 tbsp (265 mL)	granulated sugar
1 cup (250 mL)	all-purpose flour
3/4 cup (175 mL)	cornstarch
6 large	eggs, room temperature
1 tbsp (15 mL)	pure vanilla extract
4 tbsp (60 mL)	clarified melted butter, room temperature

Place sugar in a metal bowl and warm gently in a preheated 350°F (180°C) oven for about 4 minutes.

In a separate bowl, sift together flour and cornstarch; set aside.

In a third bowl, beat eggs and sugar until the eggs have tripled in volume, then add vanilla. Sift flour mixture into eggs, one-third at a time.

Fold butter into batter and smooth over a parchment-lined 12- x 18-inch (30.5 cm x 46 cm) jelly roll pan.

Bake for 25 to 30 minutes or until genoise pulls away from the pan. Invert on a clean surface and peel off parchment. Cool before using.

Ginger Genoise

This recipe, like the one for rich custard that appears earlier in this chapter, was a part of a trifle recipe I wrote for President's Choice® Magazine.

1/2 cup (125 mL)	cake and pastry flour
2 tbsp (25 mL) + 1/4 cup (50 mL)	granulated sugar
2 tsp (10 mL)	ginger
3	eggs
1/2 tsp (2 mL)	pure vanilla extract
2 tbsp (25 mL)	unsalted butter, melted and warm

Preheat oven to 350°F (180°C). Line a 15- x 10-inch (2 L) jelly roll pan with parchment paper.

In a bowl, sift together flour, 2 tbsp (25 mL) sugar and ginger; set aside. In a separate bowl, beat eggs, remaining sugar and vanilla in a heatproof bowl set over hot, not boiling, water, until mixture is pale in color, has tripled in volume and is thick enough to leave a trail when a spoon is pulled through the batter (about 6 minutes). Remove bowl from heat.

Sift dry ingredients over egg mixture and fold until incorporated. Fold in warm butter, then pour into jelly roll pan and smooth top. There will be just enough batter to cover the pan.

Bake for 8 minutes or until golden. Cake should spring back to the touch.

Let cool in pan set on a cooling rack.

Ladyfingers

This is a variation on the European sponge, or genoise, which is piped into "fingers." Ladyfingers are perfect for icebox cakes like the ones on pages 32 and 60 or the Tiramisu on page 159.

6	eggs, separated
3/4 cup (175 mL)	granulated sugar
1 tsp (5 mL)	pure vanilla extract
1 1/4 cups (300 mL)	all-purpose flour, sifted twice
1/4 tsp (1 mL)	cream of tartar
1/2 cup (125 mL)	icing sugar

Beat yolks with half the sugar until a thick ribbon falls from the beater when it is lifted. Beat in vanilla. Sift flour over yolks and fold in gently.

In a clean glass or stainless steel bowl, beat egg whites with cream of tartar, on low speed, until they begin to take shape. Increase speed to high and gradually beat in remaining sugar until whites are stiff.

Fold whites into yolks and flour in thirds.

Quickly spoon into a piping bag and pipe 3-inch (7 cm) fingers onto parchment-lined baking sheet. Dust with icing sugar.

Bake in preheated 350°F (180°C) oven for 10 minutes or until golden.

Alternatively, you can pipe the batter into an 8- or 9-inch (20 or 22 cm) drawn circle on the parchment, bake for 12 to 15 minutes and use as a cake base.

Makes 3 dozen cookies.

Nutted Meringue Rounds

These versatile rounds can be layered with buttercream or whipped cream,
spread with fruit sauces and drizzled with chocolate or syrup.

1 1/3 cups (325 mL)	shelled nuts
1 1/2 cups (375 mL)	icing sugar, sifted
5	egg whites
1/4 tsp (1 mL)	cream of tartar
1/3 cup (75 mL)	fruit sugar or granulated sugar
	processed in a blender until fine
3 tbsp (50 mL)	milk

Line a large baking sheet with parchment paper.

Use an 8-inch (1.2 L) cake pan to draw two circles on the parchment, several inches apart and away from the edges of the pan; the meringue will expand as it bakes.

Using a food processor, process half the nuts with half the icing sugar until fine. Whisk in remaining sugar.

In a clean stainless steel or glass bowl, beat egg whites with cream of tartar at low speed until they begin to firm; increase speed to high and beat until stiff peaks form. Whip in fruit sugar.

Stir milk into sugar/nut combination. Whisk in one-quarter of the meringue; then fold in remaining meringue.

Immediately fill a plain-tipped pastry bag with meringue mixture. Starting in the center of each circle, pipe a spiral to cover the ring.

Bake in a preheated 275°F (130°C) oven for 1 1/2 to 2 hours, until firm and dry, turning the pan after first hour. Turn off the oven and let cool in the oven with the door ajar.

Store uncovered at room temperature.

Makes two 8-inch rounds.

Caramel Crunch Topping for Angel Food Cake

Therese Taylor is a driving force behind the Toronto chapter of the Women's Culinary Network. She writes, "As co-owner of Dan T's Inferno Foods, I usually reserve my creativity in the kitchen for savory dishes, so when I do make a dessert, it has to be simple. My boys and I really enjoy making this topping for store-bought angel food cakes, which are inevitably devoured in one sitting."

1 cup (250 mL)	dark brown sugar
3/4 cup (175 mL)	corn syrup
1/2 cup (125 mL)	butter, melted
1 cup (250 mL)	table cream
1 tsp (5 mL)	pure vanilla extract

In a heavy-bottomed saucepan, mix together sugar, syrup, butter and cream. Bring to a boil over medium heat, stirring continually. (Lower heat if mixture starts to boil over.) Continue to cook for about 15 minutes or until the mixture reaches thread stage (230°F/110°C) on a candy thermometer.

Drizzle half the mixture over angel food cake. Return remaining mixture to medium heat and continue to boil until it reaches 330°F (162°C), about 5 minutes. Remove from heat and stir in vanilla.

Pour into a lightly greased pan and let set for 30 minutes. When hard, wrap in parchment paper and smash into tiny pieces. Sprinkle hard toffee bits onto caramel-topped angel food cake.

Makes about 1 1/2 cups (375 mL).

Caramel

Caramel's rich flavor and lovely, deep golden color are prized in the dessert kitchen. Caramel is also very simple to prepare. A word of caution when working with caramel: It is unbelievably hot.

| 2 cups (500 mL) | granulated sugar |
| 1/2 cup (125 mL) | water |

In a heavy-bottomed pot, heat sugar and water over high heat until syrup begins to turn golden. Do not stir. Watch carefully as syrup turns a darker golden then remove from heat and plunge pot into ice water.

Immediately drizzle over anything for a crunchy caramel coating.

Or pour caramel onto a flat parchment-lined surface and let harden, then break into shards for decoration. Wrap in cloth and break into tiny gems for decorating.

Or drizzle over a parchment-lined bowl and let harden; remove parchment to reveal a caramel cage.

Makes about 1 cup (250 mL).

Chocolate Espresso Mousse

This rich mousse is ideal sandwiched between genoise or crunchy meringue.

2 cups (500 mL)	whipping cream
2	eggs, separated
8 oz (240 g)	bittersweet chocolate
1/2 cup (125 mL)	granulated sugar
1/4 cup (50 mL)	water
2	egg yolks
1/3 cup (75 mL)	brewed espresso coffee
2 tbsp (25 mL)	orange liqueur or juice
6 tbsp (90 mL)	unsalted butter, room temperature

Whip cream until stiff. In a clean glass or stainless steel bowl, beat egg whites on low speed until they begin to take shape. Increase speed to high and gradually beat until whites are stiff.

Melt chocolate over hot, not boiling, water, or uncovered in a microwave on medium power; set aside.

Mix sugar with water in a saucepan and bring to a boil; boil for 3 to 4 minutes, until the syrup coats the back of a spoon.

Beat the egg yolks on high speed while slowly adding the sugar syrup in a thin stream. Beat for 7 minutes, until the mixture is thick and creamy.

Add the espresso, liqueur and butter and beat until smooth. Stir in the melted chocolate. Whip in egg whites until smooth. Fold in whipped cream.

Pour into oiled cake ring or mold and refrigerate for at least 6 hours.

Makes 5 cups (1.25 L).

Pourable Chocolate Ganache

This ganache is perfect for icing or dipping.

1 cup (250 mL)	whipping cream
8 oz (240 g)	semisweet or bittersweet chocolate, finely chopped

Heat whipping cream in a medium saucepan over medium heat until just below the boiling point.

Remove from heat, stir in chocolate until melted, then beat until completely smooth, about 10 seconds.

Let cool until the consistency is right for pouring, about 1 hour. If the chocolate becomes too thick, it can be reheated for a few seconds in the microwave or over a double boiler until pourable.

Makes 1 1/2 cups (375 mL).

Whipped Chocolate Ganache

Whipped ganache makes an unbeatable filling or frosting.

2 cups (500 mL)	whipping cream
8 oz (240 g)	semisweet or bittersweet chocolate, finely chopped

Heat whipping cream in a medium saucepan over medium heat until just below the boiling point.

Remove from heat, stir in chocolate until melted, then beat until smooth, about 10 seconds.

Chill for 1 1/2 hours and then beat at high speed until peaks form.

Makes 3 1/2 cups (875 mL).

Canada's Favorite: Chocolate Cake

Chocolate, heavenly chocolate. We just can't seem to get enough of it. Dark chocolate, white chocolate, bittersweet, semisweet and milk chocolate all tickle our fancy. Chocolate cakes can be dense, rich and flourless, or layered butter cakes with mounds of chocolate curls on top. Others are made of light and airy mousse sandwiched between crunchy meringue. You just can't beat chocolate.

During my days at The Senator Restaurant in Toronto, the one cake that never wavered in popularity was their chocolate cake made headier still with a generous helping of bourbon. Other flavors that are perfect with chocolate include coffee, of course, nuts, caramel, cream, mint, orange and berries. As I write this, I'm finishing a piece of chocolate espresso cake and feeling euphoric, inspired not only by caffeine, cocoa and sugar, but also by the wonderful taste, the moist texture and the satisfying decadence. To have cake is a lovely thing; to have chocolate cake approaches the sublime.

Flourless Chocolate Cake

I love this cake for its richness, sinful texture and simplicity.

CAKE

8 oz (230 g)	bittersweet chocolate, chopped
1/3 cup (75 mL)	coffee liqueur
1 tsp (5 mL)	pure vanilla extract
8	eggs, separated
1 cup (250 mL)	superfine sugar

ASSEMBLY

1 cup (250 mL)	orange marmalade
1 cup (250 mL)	whipping cream
1 tbsp (15 mL)	granulated sugar

For cake: Butter a 10-inch (3 L) springform pan, dust with flour and line bottom with parchment paper.

Melt chocolate with liqueur and vanilla in a double boiler or stainless steel bowl over hot, not boiling, water.

Beat egg yolks with 1/2 cup (125 mL) sugar until a thick ribbon falls from the beater when lifted.

In a clean glass or stainless steel bowl, beat egg whites with remaining sugar until stiff peaks form.

Fold chocolate mixture into egg yolks, then gently fold in egg whites.

Pour into prepared pan and bake on the middle rack at 350°F (180°C) for 40 minutes or until a tester comes out clean.

Cool in pan for at least 1 hour.

To assemble: Melt orange marmalade over low heat and spoon onto dessert plates. Whip cream with sugar until stiff. Place a slice of cooled cake over marmalade and garnish with whipped cream.

Chocolate Barley Cake

Donna Hamilton of Hamilton's Barley Flour in Olds, Alberta, came up with this recipe. Barley flour and canola oil are both healthy food choices, making this a chocolate cake you don't have to feel too guilty about.

2 cups (500 mL)	granulated sugar
2	eggs
2 tsp (10 mL)	pure vanilla extract
2/3 cup (150 mL)	canola oil
3 cups (750 mL)	whole barley flour
2/3 cup (150 mL)	cocoa
2 tsp (10 mL)	baking powder
2 tsp (10 mL)	baking soda
1 tsp (5 mL)	salt
2 cups (500 mL)	boiling water

In a large bowl, beat sugar, eggs, vanilla and oil for 4 minutes or until very light.

In a separate bowl, combine barley flour, cocoa, baking powder, baking soda and salt.

Mix dry ingredients and boiling water into egg mixture alternately, one-third of the flour mixture and half of the boiling water at a time, beginning and ending with dry ingredients. Beat until smooth.

Pour into a greased 13- x 9-inch (3.5 L) pan.

Bake on the middle rack at 350°F (180°C) for 45 minutes or until center springs back to the touch.

Remove from pan and cool on a rack. Frost with your favorite icing.

Decadent Chocolate Espresso Cake

This cake is a fabulous example of that perfect food combination:
coffee and chocolate. Who could ask for anything more?

CAKE

3/4 cup (175 mL)	cocoa
1 cup (250 mL)	very hot, brewed espresso
2 cups (500 mL)	sifted all-purpose flour
1 cup (250 mL)	sifted cake and pastry flour
1 1/2 tsp (7 mL)	baking soda
1/2 tsp (2 mL)	salt
3/4 cup (175 mL)	cold water
1/2 cup (125 mL)	plain yogurt
1 tsp (5 mL)	pure vanilla extract
3/4 cup (175 mL)	unsalted butter
2 2/3 cups (575 mL)	granulated sugar
3 large	eggs

FROSTING

3/4 cup (175 mL)	whipping cream
1/3 cup (75 mL)	strong, brewed espresso
24 oz (750 mL)	milk chocolate chunks
6 tbsp (90 mL)	unsalted butter, cubed
1 tsp (5 mL)	pure vanilla extract
pinch	salt
	chocolate-covered espresso beans, for garnish

For cake: In a bowl, stir cocoa into hot espresso until dissolved, then cool to room temperature.

In another bowl, sift together flours, baking soda and salt twice, then stir with a wire whisk.

Stir cold water, yogurt and vanilla into espresso mixture.

In a separate bowl, cream together butter and sugar until light and fluffy, then beat in eggs, one at a time.

Stir flour mixture and espresso mixture into creamed mixture alternately, one-third of the flour mixture and one half of the espresso mixture at a time, beginning and ending with flour.

Turn batter into 3 greased and parchment-lined 9-inch (1.5 L) baking pans and level.

Bake on the middle rack at 350°F (180°C) for 30 minutes or until a tester comes out clean. If pans are very close together in the oven, prohibiting free air circulation, bake in batches.

Cool for 10 minutes, then remove cakes from pans. Peel away parchment. Let cool completely.

For frosting: Heat cream and espresso over medium heat. Remove from heat, then stir in remaining ingredients until smooth.

Refrigerate for a half hour, then beat until light and spreadable.

To assemble: Spread frosting between layers and over top and sides of cake. Arrange espresso beans in 3 concentric circles on top of cake.

Milk Chocolate Chip Cookie Cake

Chocolate chip cookies add a little crunch to this moist cake.

CAKE		FROSTING	
1/2 cup (125 mL)	dutched cocoa	1 1/4 cups (300 mL)	whipping cream
1/2 cup (125 mL)	hot water	1/4 cup (50 mL)	unsalted butter
1 3/4 cups (425 mL)	all-purpose flour	2 1/2 cups (650 mL)	milk chocolate chips
2 tsp (10 mL)	baking powder	12	chocolate chip cookies, crumbled
1/2 tsp (2 mL)	baking soda		
1/4 tsp (1 mL)	salt		
1/2 cup (125 mL)	unsalted butter		
1 1/2 cups (375 mL)	granulated sugar		
3 large	eggs		
1 tsp (5 mL)	pure vanilla extract		
2/3 cup (150 mL)	homogenized milk		

For cake: Dissolve cocoa in hot water and cool to room temperature.

In a large bowl, sift together flour, baking powder, baking soda and salt. Stir with a wire whisk.

In a separate bowl, cream together butter and sugar until light and fluffy. Beat in eggs, one at a time, then vanilla and cocoa mixture.

Stir in flour mixture and milk alternately, beginning and ending with the flour.

Turn batter into 2 greased and parchment-lined 9-inch (1.5 L) cake pans and level. Bake on the middle rack at 350°F (180°C) for 35 minutes or until a tester comes out clean.

Let cool for 10 minutes, run a knife around the sides of the pans to loosen cakes and invert onto racks. Peel off parchment and allow to cool.

For frosting: Heat cream and butter over medium heat. Remove from heat and stir in chocolate chips until smooth. Chill for 5 minutes, then beat until light and spreadable.

To assemble: Spread frosting on first layer and cover with half of crumbled cookies. Place second layer on top, frost and cover with remaining crumbled cookies.

The Senator's Chocolate Cake

Anne Hollyer of The Senator Restaurant in Toronto advises that ganache must be just the right temperature or it won't coat correctly. Ganache that is too cold won't pour and ganache that is too hot won't adhere to the cake. However, if you find the ganache does pool around the cake, pour the ganache back into a container, let it cool and thicken, then try again.

1 cup (250 mL)	butter, softened
2 cups (500 mL)	granulated sugar
3	eggs, room temperature
1 cup (250 mL)	espresso coffee, room temperature
3/4 cup (175 mL)	bourbon
1/2 cup (125 mL)	coffee, room temperature
2 cups (500 mL)	all-purpose flour
1 tsp (5 mL)	baking soda
5 oz (150 g)	unsweetened chocolate, melted
1 recipe	pourable chocolate ganache (see page 18)
8	small whole strawberries, stems attached, for garnish

Beat butter for 5 minutes or until light, then cream in sugar until very pale and fluffy.

Beat eggs in one at a time.

Combine espresso, bourbon and coffee and combine flour and baking soda. Mix espresso mixture and flour mixture into egg mixture alternately, one-third of the flour mixture and half of the espresso mixture at a time, beginning and ending with dry ingredients.

Stir in melted chocolate and turn into a greased and floured 10-inch (2.5 L) bundt pan.

Bake on the middle rack at 350°F (180°C) for 1 hour or until the center springs back to the touch.

Cool on a rack for 10 minutes, then invert to remove from pan.

Let cake cool, then pour ganache over the top to coat. Dip whole strawberries in ganache and place atop cake for garnish.

Chocolate Layer Cake

This triple-layer cake can be served with a plain frosting or can be further decorated with large chocolate curls, white chocolate curls or a combination of both.

1 1/2 cups (375 mL)	butter
2 cups (500 mL)	granulated sugar
4	eggs
1 tbsp (15 mL)	pure vanilla extract
3/4 cup (175 mL)	cocoa
1 1/2 cups (375 mL)	boiling water (or coffee)
3 1/2 cups (875 mL)	all-purpose flour
1 1/2 tbsp (22 mL)	baking powder
1 tsp (5 mL)	baking soda
1 tsp (5 mL)	salt
1 1/2 recipes	chocolate buttercream (see page 5)

In a large bowl, mix butter on high speed until very light. Cream in sugar until light and fluffy. Beat in eggs, one at a time, fully incorporating after each addition. Beat in vanilla.

In a small bowl, dissolve cocoa in hot water; cool.

Whisk together flour, baking powder, baking soda and salt.

Stir flour mixture and cocoa mixture into creamed mixture alternately, one-third of the flour mixture and half of the cocoa mixture at a time, beginning and ending with dry ingredients.

Turn into 3 greased, parchment-lined 9-inch (1.5 L) cake pans and bake on the middle rack at 350°F (180°C) for 25 to 30 minutes or until a tester comes out clean.

Remove from pans after 5 to 10 minutes and let cool completely.

Fill and frost with chocolate buttercream.

Chocolate Pistachio Torte

A friend described to me the best cake she had ever tasted: a moist butter cake, layered with sweet buttercream, offset by crunchy pistachios. From her description, I invented this cake.

1 1/2 cups (375 mL)	unsalted butter, softened
1 1/2 cups (375 mL)	granulated sugar
4	eggs, room temperature
2 cups (500 mL)	all-purpose flour
2 tsp (10 mL)	baking powder
1/2 tsp (2 mL)	salt
4 oz (120 g)	semisweet chocolate
2 tbsp (25 mL)	chocolate or hazelnut liqueur
1 tsp (5 mL)	pure vanilla extract
2 cups (500 mL)	ground pistachios
3 cups (750 mL)	chocolate buttercream (see recipe on page 5)
1 cup (250 mL)	whole shelled pistachios

Beat butter on high speed until very light. Cream in sugar until light and fluffy. Beat eggs in one at time, making sure they are fully mixed in after each addition.

In another bowl, whisk together flour, baking powder and salt.

Melt chocolate over hot, not boiling, water or in a microwave, uncovered, on medium. Stir liqueur and vanilla into melted chocolate.

Stir flour mixture into creamed mixture, then fold in chocolate mixture and 1 cup (250 mL) of the ground nuts.

Turn into 2 greased and floured 9-inch (1.5 mL) cake pans and bake on the middle rack at 350°F (180°C) for 30 to 35 minutes or until a tester comes out clean.

Cool for 10 minutes, then remove from cakes from pans. Let cool completely.

To assemble: Fill and frost cake with chocolate buttercream. Press remaining ground nuts into sides of cake and garnish top with whole pistachio nuts.

Rich Chocolate Cake

This recipe originates with chef-instructor Sandra Cranston-Corradini, who trained at the Cordon Bleu School of Cookery in England, the Beverley Burge School of Cooking in Toronto and the New Orleans School of Cooking. She mastered Thai vegetable carving at Bangkok Gardens and studied fine foods with caterers in Belgium, Switzerland and the former Soviet Union. For the past 13 years she has been principal of The Cranston-Corradini School of Cooking, and she is currently a writer for In the Hills magazine.

CAKE

1 cup + 3 tbsp (300 mL)	salted butter
7 oz (200 g)	semisweet chocolate
2 oz (60 g)	bittersweet chocolate
1 cup (250 mL)	granulated sugar
1/2 cup (125 mL)	brown sugar
6	eggs, separated
1/3 cup (75 mL)	cake and pastry flour
2 tbsp (25 mL)	ground almonds
1/2 tsp (2 mL)	cream of tartar

CHOCOLATE SAUCE

6 oz (170 g)	semisweet or dark chocolate
10 oz (284 g)	water
2/3 cup (150 mL)	granulated sugar

CHOCOLATE MOUSSE

6 oz (170 g)	semisweet chocolate
2 1/2 oz (71 g)	espresso
1 1/2 tbsp (22 mL)	unsalted butter
1/2 oz (14 g)	rum or liqueur of choice
3	eggs, separated

For cake: Line a 10-inch (1.8 L) round pan with parchment, then grease and flour it. Melt butter, semisweet chocolate and bittersweet chocolate and then set aside.

Beat granulated sugar and brown sugar into yolks until just mixed, and whisk into warm chocolate mixture. Stir in flour and almonds.

In a clean glass or stainless steel bowl, beat egg whites and cream of tartar to soft peaks. Quickly fold whites into chocolate mixture.

Bake at 375°F (190°C) for 30 to 40 minutes or until set around sides. The center should still wiggle slightly when the pan is shaken. Run a palette knife around the edges to release, but do not attempt to turn out. Cool in pan with a damp cloth over top.

For sauce: Chop chocolate and combine with water and sugar in a medium-sized, heavy-bottomed saucepan, and gently melt. When chocolate has melted, simmer for 15 minutes. Remove from heat. (This sauce may be served hot or cold. Any extra may be frozen.)

For mousse: Chop chocolate and melt with espresso and butter. Remove from heat and add liqueur. While still hot, stir in egg yolks one at a time.

In a clean glass or stainless steel bowl, beat egg whites to soft peaks and fold into the chocolate mixture.

To assemble: Make a parchment paper collar to go around the cake and secure with kitchen twine. Pour mousse over top. Let set for 2 days. Remove parchment paper collar and serve cake with chocolate sauce.

Chocolate Mousse Cake

For me, the best chocolate mousse is achieved by layering the flavors of chocolate and coffee, cream and liqueur. This cake strikes a wonderful balance of these tastes, wrapped up in a sensuous, smooth-textured dessert.

CAKE				
2 recipes	genoise (see page 11)		3/4 cup (175 mL)	milk
1/2 cup (125 mL)	orange, hazelnut or chocolate liqueur		1 cup (250 mL)	granulated sugar
			6	egg yolks
MOUSSE			4 squares	bittersweet chocolate
1 envelope	unflavored gelatin		1/4 cup (50 mL)	brewed espresso
1 tbsp (15 mL)	warm water		3 cups (750 mL)	whipping cream
				chocolate curls or shaved chocolate, for garnish

For cake: Cut four 9-inch (23 cm) circles from genoise. Brush cooled cake with liqueur.

For mousse: In a bowl, dissolve gelatin in warm water.

In a small saucepan, heat milk until it begins to simmer.

Using another bowl, whip sugar and egg yolks until a thick ribbon falls when the beater is lifted. Slowly whip the hot milk into the yolks; return to the heat, whisking constantly until it thickens, then remove from heat. Whisk in gelatin, then beat until light and thick.

Melt chocolate with the espresso in a stainless steel bowl over hot, not boiling, water, or uncovered in a microwave on medium. Whip into mixture.

Whip cream until thick, then fold approximately two-thirds of whipped cream into chocolate mixture.

To assemble: Use a 9-inch (2.5 L) springform pan to assemble cake. Layer as follows: cake, half of chocolate mixture, cake, one-third of the remaining whipped cream, cake, remaining chocolate mixture, whipped cream, cake, remaining whipped cream.

Chill, refrigerated, overnight.

Garnish with chocolate curls or shaved chocolate.

Chocolate Coffee Cake

Grandma would serve this invigorating cake for breakfast on the mornings that my brother, sister and I had slept over. Three kids hopped up on chocolate and coffee were her special present for my parents.

CAKE		TOPPING	
3 oz (90 g)	semisweet chocolate	2/3 cup (150 mL)	all-purpose flour
1/2 cup (125 mL)	brewed coffee	2/3 cup (150 mL)	chopped pecans
1/2 cup (125 mL)	milk, room temperature	2/3 cup (150 mL)	light brown sugar
2 cups (500 mL)	all-purpose flour	4 tsp (20 mL)	salt
1 tsp (5 mL)	baking powder	1/3 cup (75 mL)	unsalted butter, melted
1 tsp (5 mL)	baking soda		
1/4 tsp (1 mL)	salt		
4 tbsp (60 mL)	unsalted butter, softened		
1/2 cup (125 mL)	granulated sugar		
2 large	eggs		

For cake: Melt chocolate in a bowl over hot, not boiling, water. Add coffee and milk. Set aside 2 tbsp (25 mL) of this mixture for topping.

For topping: Combine flour, pecans, brown sugar and salt. Whisk in unsalted butter and 2 tbsp (25 mL) of coffee mixture.

Press topping into the bottom of a greased 9-inch (3 L) fluted tube pan.

For cake: Combine flour, baking powder, baking soda and salt.

In a separate bowl, cream together butter and sugar; beat in eggs and add coffee mixture. Stir flour into wet ingredients in thirds and mix until smooth. Pour cake batter over topping. Bake on middle rack at 350°F (180°C) for 40 minutes or until a tester comes out clean.

Chocolate Icebox Cake

This cake is fairly easy to make and offers many decorating opportunities. It's pretty enough to serve simply topped with whipped cream or white or dark chocolate curls or shavings. A contrasting white Italian meringue border would look nice, as would wrapping the cake in a wide strip of chocolate taller than the cake, then gently folding in the edges.

2 cups (500 mL)	whipping cream		2 tbsp (25 mL)	orange liqueur
8 oz (230 g)	bittersweet chocolate		6 tbsp (90 mL)	unsalted butter, room temperature
1/2 cup (125 mL)	granulated sugar			
1/4 cup (50 mL)	water		3 dozen	ladyfingers
2	eggs, separated			(purchased or made from
2	egg yolks			recipe on page 13) or
1/3 cup (75 mL)	brewed espresso		5 dozen	vanilla wafers

Whip cream until stiff.

Melt chocolate over hot, not boiling, water, or uncovered in a microwave on medium power.

Mix sugar with water in a saucepan and bring to a boil; boil for 3 to 4 minutes or until the syrup coats the back of a spoon.

Beat the 4 egg yolks on high speed while slowly adding the sugar syrup in a thin stream. Beat for 7 minutes, until the mixture is thick and creamy. Add the espresso, liqueur and butter and beat until smooth. Stir in the melted chocolate.

In a clean glass or stainless steel bowl, beat egg whites until stiff. Whisk into the chocolate mixture, then fold in the whipped cream.

Place a layer of cookies in the bottom of a parchment-lined 9-inch (2.5 L) springform pan. Pour in one-third of the chocolate mousse. Arrange cookies around the sides of the pan, and place a second layer of cookies gently over the chocolate mousse. Pour in another one-third of the chocolate mousse. Place a final layer of cookies over top and finish with chocolate mousse.

Refrigerate for 4 hours or overnight to set. Release springform and remove outer ring.

Chocolate Pecan Meringue Cake

Light, crunchy meringue layers are filled with chocolate buttercream to create this simple, sophisticated cake. I like to serve it alongside a snifter of cognac and a small espresso.

1 cup (250 mL)	toasted pecans
1 1/2 cups (375 mL)	icing sugar, sifted
5	egg whites
1/4 tsp (1 mL)	cream of tartar
1/3 cup (75 mL)	fruit sugar or sugar processed in a food processor until fine
3 tbsp (50 mL)	milk
1 recipe	chocolate buttercream (see page 5)

Line a large baking sheet with parchment paper. Use an 8-inch (1.2 L) cake pan or cake ring to draw two circles on the parchment, several inches apart and away from the edges of the pan; meringue will expand as it bakes.

Using a food processor, process half the pecans with half the icing sugar until fine. Whisk in remaining sugar.

In a clean stainless steel or glass bowl, beat egg whites with cream of tartar at low speed until they begin to firm; increase speed to high and beat until stiff peaks form. Whip in fruit sugar.

Stir milk into sugar/pecan mixture. Whisk in one-quarter of the meringue, then fold in remaining meringue.

Fill a plain-tipped pastry bag with meringue; then, starting in the center of each circle, pipe a spiral that covers the ring.

Bake at 275°F (130°C) for 1 1/2 to 2 hours, turning the pan after the first hour, or until firm and dry. Turn off the oven and let cool in the oven with the door ajar.

To assemble: Spread chocolate buttercream over the bottom meringue (choose the most uneven of the two) and sprinkle with half of the remaining nuts. Cover with top meringue and press down lightly but firmly. Spread remaining buttercream over top and sides of cake. Sprinkle remaining nuts along the edge of the top of the cake.

Chocolate Banana Cake

Pistachios have been eaten since 7000 BCE, but this may well be the best use yet found for them. Paired with chocolate, they fill this moist banana cake.

1 1/2 cups (375 mL)	all-purpose flour
2 tsp (10 mL)	baking powder
pinch	salt
1/2 cup (125 mL)	butter
1/2 cup (125 mL)	granulated sugar
3 large	eggs, separated
1 cup (250 mL)	ripe banana (about 3 bananas)
1/4 cup (50 mL)	milk
2 tsp (10 mL)	pure vanilla extract
1 recipe	chocolate buttercream (see page 5)
1 1/4 cups (300 mL)	ground pistachios, for garnish

In a large bowl, sift together flour, baking powder and salt, twice. In a separate bowl, cream together butter and sugar until light and fluffy. Beat in egg yolks, one at a time, followed by ripe banana, milk and vanilla. (Mixture may appear curdled.) Stir flour mixture into wet mixture in thirds.

In a clean stainless steel or glass bowl, whip egg whites until soft peaks form. Fold into batter.

Bake in a greased and floured 10-inch (3 L) springform pan on the middle rack at 350°F (180°C) for 30 minutes or until a tester comes out clean. Cool for 10 minutes, then remove from pan. Let cool completely on a rack, then use a serrated knife to slice cake in half horizontally.

To assemble: Fold 1/2 cup (125 mL) pistachios into one-third of the chocolate buttercream. Use that third to fill the cake. Frost the top and sides with plain chocolate buttercream. Press remaining pistachios into sides of cake.

A Piece of Cake from Quebec

The culinary traditions of Quebec are rich with all manner of gâteaux. The French passion for chocolate is reflected here, as is a penchant for walnuts, airy mousse, crispy layered meringue and liqueur-soaked genoise. Quebec's worldwide reputation for fine cuisine is in part due to stunning, elegant desserts and warm, homey regional specialties.

Writing this chapter gave me the opportunity to rummage through the recipe files of my friend, chef André Théberge. André's Quebecois roots flavored his creative cooking throughout his career, and his versions of some scrumptious cakes appear here. I was also thrilled to speak to my friends Micheline Mongrain-Dontigny and Johanne Pouliot, who have made a passion of celebrating traditional Quebecois cuisine. If you were hoping to find the Christmas classic Buche de Noel, see page 127 in "Our Professional Best."

Chocolate Walnut Torte

The next six recipes come from talented Quebecois chef André Théberge. André's talent was tremendous, combining tastes and textures with skill and grace. Sadly, André has died, but his recipes remain in my files, and it is with great pleasure that I share them.

9	eggs, room temperature
1 cup (250 mL)	granulated sugar
3/4 cup (175 mL)	all-purpose flour
2 tbsp (25 mL)	cornstarch
2 tbsp (25 mL)	cocoa
2 recipes	whipped chocolate ganache (see page 18)
3/4 cup (175 mL)	chopped walnuts, for garnish

Beat the eggs with the sugar until they have tripled in volume, about 7 minutes. Sift flour, cornstarch and cocoa together twice, then sift into eggs and fold in quickly.

Pour into two 9-inch (1.5 L) cake pans, which have been greased, floured and lined with parchment.

Bake on the middle rack at 350°F (180°C) for 20 minutes or until a tester comes out clean.

When cake is cool, slice each round in half horizontally. Spread one-quarter of the ganache over each of the four layers, stack and sprinkle with chopped walnuts.

Banana Mousse Cake

*This cake may be daunting for the beginner. If, however, you feel in the mood for
something more than a pound cake, give it a whirl. Never fear, making mousse and using
a pastry bag really aren't that difficult once you've done it a few times. And even
if you don't quite get it right, you'll have the fun of eating your mistakes.*

CAKE

3	eggs, separated, room temperature
1/2 cup (125 mL)	granulated sugar
1 tsp (5 mL)	pure vanilla extract
pinch	cream of tartar
pinch	salt
2/3 cup (150 mL)	all-purpose flour

MOUSSE

1 envelope	unflavored gelatin
1/4 cup (50 mL)	water, warm
1 1/2 cups (375 mL)	ripe, mashed banana
2 tbsp (25 mL)	lemon juice
3/4 cup (175 mL)	granulated sugar
1 1/2 cups (375 mL)	whipping cream
1/4 cup (50 mL)	ground hazelnuts, for garnish

For cake: Place a 6- x 10-inch (15 cm x 25 cm) piece of parchment onto a baking sheet.

Whisk egg yolks with 6 tbsp (90 mL) of the sugar in a stainless steel bowl over hot, not boiling,
water for 3 minutes. Beat on high speed until yolks have tripled in volume, about 6 minutes,
then beat in vanilla.

In a clean glass or stainless steel bowl, beat egg whites with cream of tartar to form soft peaks.
Beat in salt and remaining 2 tbsp (25 mL) of sugar until whites are stiff, not dry.

Sift one-third of the flour into yolk mixture and fold in one-third of whites. Repeat until mixtures are completely combined. Smooth or pipe batter over parchment paper, leaving a 1/2-inch (1 cm) border on all sides.

Bake in lower third of oven at 325°F (160°C) for 15 minutes or until cake is golden and springs back to the touch. Invert onto a cooling rack and peel off parchment.

For mousse: Dissolve gelatin in water. Puree banana with lemon juice and sugar until smooth. If using a food processor, pour in gelatin while machine is running; otherwise, whisk in gelatin until smooth.

Cover mousse and refrigerate for 30 minutes.

Whip cream. Whisk banana mixture for 2 minutes to blend, then fold in whipped cream, one-third at a time. Line a 9- x 5-inch (2 L) loaf pan with parchment paper, leaving 1 inch (2.5 cm) of paper extending over edges.

Halve cake horizontally, yielding two thin layers. Trim each layer to fit loaf pan. Spoon half of mousse into pan and cover with one layer of cake. Spoon remaining mousse over cake and cover with last layer of cake, cut side toward mousse. Cover with plastic wrap and refrigerate overnight. Invert mousse cake onto serving plate, peel off parchment and dust with hazelnuts.

André's Chocolate Layer Cake

Coffee and chocolate. I just can't seem to get enough of either, so here is another excuse to indulge in both. This cake was a favorite of diners at André's restaurant.

1 1/4 cups (300 mL)	all-purpose flour
3 tbsp (50 mL)	cocoa
1 tsp (5 mL)	baking powder
1/2 tsp (2 mL)	baking soda
1/2 tsp (2 mL)	salt
4	eggs, separated
1 tsp (5 mL)	white vinegar
2/3 cup (150 mL)	unsalted butter, room temperature
2 cups (500 mL)	brown sugar, firmly packed
2/3 cup (150 mL)	sour cream
3 tbsp (50 mL)	coffee liqueur
3 oz (90 g)	unsweetened chocolate, chopped finely
2/3 cup (150 mL)	hot coffee
1 recipe	mocha buttercream (see page 6)

Sift together flour, cocoa, baking powder, baking soda and salt, twice. Set aside.

In a clean glass or stainless steel bowl, beat egg whites for 1 minute then add vinegar, continuing to beat until whites hold their shape.

In a separate bowl, cream together butter and sugar. Add yolks, and beat well. Beat in sour cream and liqueur.

In another bowl, melt chocolate in hot coffee, then combine with sour cream mixture. Stir into flour mixture and fold in whites.

Pour into two 8-inch (1.2 L) greased and floured pans and bake on middle rack of a 350°F (180°C) oven for 35 minutes or until inserted toothpick comes out clean. Let cool.

Use a serrated knife to halve cakes horizontally. Fill and frost with mocha buttercream.

Reine de Saba

A cake fit for royalty! I like to make this cake and present it as a surprise for friends on days when they need to remember that they are a king or prince, queen or duchess.

8 oz (240 g)	bittersweet chocolate
6 tbsp (90 mL)	unsalted butter
4	eggs, separated
1/2 cup (125 mL)	granulated sugar
1/3 cup (75 mL)	espresso or orange liqueur
1/3 cup (75 mL)	almonds, toasted and ground
1/3 cup (75 mL)	cake and pastry flour, sifted

Melt chocolate and butter over hot, not boiling, water. Beat yolks and sugar together until pale yellow and thick. Stir in warm chocolate mixture and coffee or liqueur.

Using a food processor, pulse almonds and flour 2 to 3 times, then fold into chocolate mixture.

In a clean glass or stainless steel bowl, beat egg whites to soft peaks and fold into batter. Pour into a buttered, floured 9-inch (2.5 L) springform pan and bake in the lower third of a 375°F (190°C) oven for 25 minutes or until set.

Let cool in pan before serving.

Gâteau au Fromage à la Citrouille

*This cheesecake is baked in a water bath to ensure slow, even baking.
Cool the cake in the oven with the door propped open slightly. All this trouble
will be rewarded with a wonderful creamy texture.*

1 1/2 lbs (750 g)	cream cheese, room temperature
1 cup (250 mL)	granulated sugar
3	eggs +
1	yolk, room temperature
2 tsp (10 mL)	cinnamon
1/2 cup (125 mL)	sour cream, room temperature
2 1/2 tsp (12 mL)	lemon juice, room temperature
2 tsp (10 mL)	pure vanilla extract
1 tsp (5 mL)	grated lemon zest

In a large bowl, cream together cheese and sugar until very smooth. Beat in yolk and eggs, one at a time, so each is fully incorporated before the next addition. Beat in cinnamon, then sour cream, lemon juice, vanilla and lemon zest.

Pour into a greased, parchment-lined 10-inch (3 L) pan that has been wrapped with foil. Place in a larger pan with 1 inch (2.5 cm) of very hot water.

Bake in the middle of a 300°F (150°C) oven for 1 hour. Allow the cake to cool in the oven with the heat off and the door propped open.

Cover and refrigerate for several hours or overnight before removing from pan.

Chocolate Cheesecake

*To avoid the cracking that results when cheesecake is overbaked,
I recommend a low oven temperature. Confirm the temperature of
your oven with an oven thermometer.*

CRUST

1 1/4 cups (300 mL)	chocolate cookie crumbs
1/3 cup (75 mL)	unsalted butter, melted

CAKE

1 lb (500 g)	cream cheese
1/2 cup (125 mL)	granulated sugar
3	eggs
1/3 cup (75 mL)	almond liqueur
1 tsp (5 mL)	pure vanilla extract
6 oz (180 g)	semisweet chocolate
2/3 cup (150 mL)	sour cream

SAUCE

1/2 cup (125 mL)	cream
1/2 cup (125 mL)	semisweet chocolate chips or shavings
1/2 cup (125 mL)	slivered almonds, for garnish

For crust: Combine crumbs and melted butter, then press into a parchment-lined 9-inch (2.5 L) springform pan.

For cake: In a large bowl, blend together cream cheese and sugar until smooth. Beat in eggs, one at a time, followed by liqueur and vanilla.

Melt chocolate over hot water, then stir into sour cream. Blend sour cream mixture into cheese mixture. Pour into pan and bake on the middle rack at 300°F (150°C) for 60 minutes or until set.

Allow to cool in oven with the heat off and the door ajar for 1 hour; cover with plastic wrap and refrigerate for several hours or overnight.

For sauce: Heat cream in a saucepan and whisk in chocolate until smooth. Allow to cool, then spread over cake. Garnish with almonds.

Orange Almond Cake

*Would anyone care for a glass of chilled Pineau des Charentes? The heady aperitif
has a fragrant orange bouquet that suits this cake perfectly.*

1 1/3 cups (325 mL)	granulated sugar
6	eggs, separated
	grated zest of 2 oranges
2/3 cup (150 mL)	orange juice
1/2 tsp (2 mL)	almond extract
2 cups (500 mL)	finely ground almonds
1 1/2 cups (375 mL)	sifted cake and pastry flour
2 tsp (10 mL)	baking powder
1/2 tsp (2 mL)	cardamom
1/4 tsp (1 mL)	salt
1 cup (250 mL)	unsalted butter, melted

Cream together sugar and egg yolks until pale and ribbony. Add orange zest, juice and almond extract and beat until foamy.

Combine almonds, flour, baking powder, cardamom and salt, then stir into egg yolk mixture. Stir in butter.

In a clean glass or stainless steel bowl, beat egg whites until soft peaks form. Fold into batter, in thirds. Pour into 2 greased, floured 9-inch (1.5 L) cake pans and bake on the middle rack at 350°F (180°C) for 30 to 35 minutes or until a tester comes out clean.

Georgeville Raspberry and Brown Sugar Crumble Cake

Chef Steven Beyrouty, owner of the stunning and historic Auberge Georgeville in Georgeville, Quebec, polled his guests to determine which of his cakes they most admired. This cake, traditionally eaten in Germany as a late-afternoon snack with freshly whipped cream, came out on top.

CAKE		TOPPING	
1 cup (250 mL)	salted butter, softened	1/2 cup (125 mL)	salted butter, softened
1 cup (250 mL)	granulated sugar	1/2 cup (125 mL)	brown sugar
	zest and juice of 1 lemon	1 cup (250 mL)	flour
3	medium eggs		
2/3 cup (150 mL)	all-purpose flour		
1 tbsp (15 mL)	baking powder		
1/3 cup + 2 tbsp (100 mL)	milk		
1 cup (250 mL)	raspberries, fresh		

For cake: In a large bowl, cream together butter, sugar, zest, juice and eggs for 3 to 4 minutes or until very pale.

In a separate bowl, sift together flour and baking powder, then stir into creamed mixture in thirds. Slowly stir in milk. Fold in raspberries and pour into a buttered 10-inch (3 L) springform pan.

For topping: Mix topping ingredients with hands until combined but crumbly. Sprinkle crumble over the surface of the cake.

Place pan on a baking sheet and bake at 350°F (180°C) for 1 hour or until tester comes out clean.

Cool on a rack for 30 minutes before releasing the springform.

Jos Louis

This recipe comes from Micheline Mongrain-Dontigny's book, Traditional Quebec Cooking: A Treasure of Heirloom Recipes. Micheline writes, "These cakes originate from the Beauce region. The founder of a bakery, Arcade Vachon, named them after his eldest sons, Joseph and Louis."

CAKE

1/2 cup (125 mL)	shortening
1 cup (250 mL)	granulated sugar
2	eggs
1 tsp (5 mL)	pure vanilla extract
1 3/4 cups (425 mL)	all-purpose flour
2 tsp (10 mL)	baking powder
1 tsp (5 mL)	baking soda
1 tsp (5 mL)	salt
4 tsp (20 mL)	cocoa
1 cup (250 mL)	milk

FILLING

1 1/3 cups (325 mL)	butter
5 tbsp (75 mL)	boiling water
5 cups (1.25 L)	icing sugar
1 tsp (5 mL)	pure vanilla extract

For cake: In a large bowl, cream shortening, then beat in sugar. Add eggs and mix well. Add vanilla.

In a separate bowl, mix flour, baking powder, baking soda, salt and cocoa.

Mix dry ingredients and milk into egg mixture alternately, one-third of the flour mixture and half of the milk at a time, beginning and ending with dry ingredients.

Drop heaping tablespoons of cake batter onto a greased cookie sheet, leaving space for cakes to expand while cooking.

Bake at 350°F (180°C) for 8 to 10 minutes or until an inserted cake tester comes out clean.

Cool cakes on a rack.

For filling: Cream butter and mix in boiling water 1 tbsp (15 mL) at a time. Add icing sugar 1 cup (250 mL) at a time while beating constantly, then add vanilla. Filling should be thick.

Spread top of 1 cake with filling and place second cake on top.

Makes 20 cakes.

Maple Walnut Gâteau

This stylish offering is suitable for presentation at the table after an upscale dinner, or when having guests over for an evening snack.

MERINGUE

1 1/2 cups (375 mL)	icing sugar, sifted
1/2 cup (125 mL)	chopped walnuts
1 tsp (5 mL)	ginger
5	egg whites
1/4 tsp (1 mL)	cream of tartar
1/3 cup (75 mL)	fruit sugar or granulated sugar processed in a blender until fine
3 tbsp (50 mL)	milk

ASSEMBLY

1/2 recipe	buttercream (see page 3)
1/2 cup (125 mL)	maple syrup
3 oz (90 g)	white chocolate
	walnut halves, for garnish

For meringue: Line a large baking sheet with parchment paper. Draw two 8-inch (20 cm) circles on the parchment, several inches apart and away from the edges of the pan; the meringue will expand as it bakes.

Using a food processor, process half the icing sugar with walnuts until fine. Whisk in remaining sugar and ginger.

In a clean stainless steel or glass bowl, beat egg whites with cream of tartar at low speed until they begin to firm; increase speed to high and beat until stiff peaks form. Whip in fruit sugar.

Stir milk into sugar/walnut combination. Whisk in one-quarter of the meringue; then fold in remaining meringue.

Immediately fill a plain-tipped piping bag with meringue. Starting in the center of each circle, pipe a spiral to cover the ring.

Bake at 275°F (130°C) for 1 1/2 to 2 hours, turning the pan after the first hour, or until firm and dry. Turn off the oven and let cool in the oven with the door ajar.

To assemble: Spread buttercream over the bottom meringue (choose the most uneven of the two) and drizzle with half the maple syrup. Cover with top meringue and press down lightly, but firmly. Drizzle syrup over top.

Melt white chocolate over hot, not boiling, water or uncovered in the microwave on medium power and drizzle over the top and sides of the cake. Garnish with walnut halves.

Gâteau de Noisette

This cake is typical of the French influence on Canadian baking that is currently very fashionable. Genoise, a kind of foam or sponge cake, is layered with complementary fillings in many cakes of this type, while others use meringue-based layers.

1 recipe	ginger genoise (see page 12)
1/3 cup (75 mL)	hazelnut liqueur
1 recipe	rich custard (see page 9), cooled
1 cup (250 mL)	toasted sliced hazelnuts
1 recipe	European buttercream (see page 4)

Cut ginger genoise into two equal rectangles and brush with hazelnut liqueur.

Spread custard over one genoise and cover with half the hazelnuts. Top with second genoise layer.

Use European buttercream to frost top and sides of cake. Garnish with remaining hazelnuts. Chill at least 6 hours or overnight.

Cut carefully, using a large serrated knife.

A Piece of Cake from Ontario

Rhubarb, apple, elderberry and maple are the flavors of my childhood, and they are baked into the pies in this chapter, a salute to the cakes of my home province. And there is so much more. Creamy goat's cheese is baked into a pound cake, and our award-winning wine is brushed onto a tipsy cake.

The bakers in this section include the owner of a Muskoka-area B&B, a home economist, a blue ribbon winner, a few home cooks and my sweet Aunt Helen. These are the women baking on the front lines of life, for their families, their communities, their customers and their friends. Every cake they produce is a work of love and tenderness that expresses itself in balanced flavors and soft crumbs.

Tangy Orange Rhubarb Crunch Coffee Cake

Gaye Mussleman bakes this cake for her guests at Woodland Springs B&B Penlake in Muskoka. Visit her website for Mennonite- and Muskoka-inspired recipes at www.penlake-woodsprings.com. She devised this recipe to recall memories of neighborhood moms handing out paper cones filled with brown sugar, cinnamon, sweet raisins and orange zest, which the children would take into the rhubarb patch. The rhubarb was snapped from the plant and dipped in the cone for a healthy treat.

CAKE

2 cups (500 mL)	sifted all-purpose flour
1 tsp (5 mL)	baking powder
2 tsp (10 mL)	baking soda
1/2 tsp (2 mL)	freshly ground nutmeg
1/2 tsp (2 mL)	allspice
1 tbsp (15 mL)	cinnamon
1/2 cup (125 mL)	shortening
1 1/2 cups (375 mL)	granulated sugar
2	eggs, beaten
2 tsp (10 mL)	pure vanilla extract
1/2 cup	orange juice concentrate
1/2 cup (125 mL)	light raisins
	zest of 1 large orange
1	orange, peeled and thinly sliced
2 cups (500 mL)	diced rhubarb
1 cup (250 mL)	sour cream

FILLING/TOPPING

1/4 cup (50 mL)	butter
1/3 cup (75 mL)	brown sugar
1/4 cup (50 mL)	granulated sugar
1 tsp (5 mL)	cinnamon
1 cup (250 mL)	chopped walnuts

RIVELS

1/2 cup (125 mL)	brown sugar
1/2 cup (125 mL)	flour
3 tbsp (50 mL)	butter

For cake: Combine flour, baking powder, baking soda, nutmeg, allspice and cinnamon in a large bowl.

In a separate bowl, cream together shortening and 1 cup (250 mL) sugar. Beat in eggs and vanilla.

In a medium saucepan, combine orange juice concentrate, raisins, zest, orange and remaining 1/2 cup (125 mL) of sugar; simmer until raisins are plumped and all the liquid is absorbed. Stir in rhubarb.

Mix dry ingredients and sour cream into egg mixture alternately, one-third of the flour mixture and half the sour cream at a time, beginning and ending with dry ingredients. Fold in orange-raisin mixture.

For filling/topping: In a small saucepan, melt butter, then stir in brown sugar, granulated sugar, cinnamon and walnuts.

For rivels: Stir together sugar and flour, then rub in butter with fingertips until crumbly.

Place half the batter in an oiled 10-inch (3 L) springform pan and sprinkle half filling over, then cover with remaining batter. Cover first with rivels and then remaining topping.

Bake on the middle rack at 350°F (180°C) for 1 hour or until a tester comes out clean. Cool in pan.

Glazed Apple Bundt Cake

Make this cake with fresh apples from Ontario's fall harvest.

3 cups (750 mL)	all-purpose flour
2 tsp (10 mL)	cinnamon
1 tsp (5 mL)	freshly ground nutmeg
1 tsp (5 mL)	ginger
1 tsp (5 mL)	baking soda
1/4 tsp (1 mL)	salt
2 cups (500 mL)	granulated sugar
1 1/2 cups (375 mL)	vegetable oil
3	large eggs
1 tsp (5 mL)	vanilla
3 cups (750 mL)	diced apples
1 cup (250 mL)	ground walnuts
2 recipes	basic glaze (see page 7)

Sift together flour, cinnamon, nutmeg, ginger, baking soda and salt, twice. Stir together with a wire whisk.

In another bowl, beat together sugar and oil, then beat in eggs, one at a time. Stir in vanilla.

Coat apples in 1/3 cup of flour mixture, then, in thirds, gently stir flour mixture, apples and walnuts into egg mixture.

Turn into a greased and floured 10-inch (2.5 L) bundt pan and bake on the middle rack at 325°F (160°C) for 1 hour and 20 minutes or until a tester comes out clean.

Cool for 10 minutes then remove from pan and brush with warm glaze 5 times.

Niagara Tipsy Cake

Dessert wines from the world-renowned vineyards of the Niagara Peninsula are ideally suited to this English classic. Chill remaining wine to enjoy with the cake.

CAKE		ASSEMBLY	
1 1/2 cups (375 mL)	all-purpose flour	1/2 cup (125 mL)	dessert wine
1 1/2 tsp (7 mL)	baking powder	1/2 cup +	
1/4 tsp (2 mL)	salt	2 tbsp (150 mL)	peach jam
1/2 cup +		1 recipe	Troy's custard, chilled (see page 10)
2 tbsp (150 mL)	unsalted butter,		
1/2 cup (125 mL)	granulated sugar		
2	large eggs +		
1	yolk		
1 tsp (5 mL)	pure vanilla extract		
3/4 cup (175 mL)	milk		

For cake: Sift together flour, baking powder and salt, then stir with a wire whisk.

In another bowl, cream together butter and sugar until light and fluffy. Beat in eggs, one at a time, then yolk, then vanilla.

Mix dry ingredients and milk into egg mixture alternately, one-third of the flour mixture and half the milk at a time, beginning and ending with dry ingredients.

Pour into two 9-inch (1.5 L) parchment-lined pans that have been greased and floured.

Bake on the middle rack at 350°F (180°C) for 20 minutes or until a tester comes out clean.

Cool for 5 minutes, then remove from pan and cool.

To assemble: Halve each cake horizontally. Brush bottom round with one-quarter of the wine, then smooth one-third jam over top.

Repeat with each layer until the final layer sits on top, cut side down. Brush top with dessert wine, then frost top and sides with custard.

Joan's Cheesecake

Home economist Joan Ttooulias has had great success with this creamy cheesecake.
She notes that cheesecake ages well and can be made up to 5 days before being served.
Take note of her terrific method for fast coulis.

CRUST

1 1/2 cups (375 mL)	crushed digestive biscuits (approx. 24 biscuits)
1/4 cup (50 mL)	finely chopped pecans or almonds, optional
1/4 cup (50 mL)	granulated sugar
1 tsp (5 mL)	cinnamon, optional
1/2 cup (125 mL)	melted butter

CHEESECAKE

2 lb (1 kg)	cream cheese
1 cup (250 mL)	granulated sugar
6	eggs
1/2 cup (125 mL)	table cream
2 tbsp (25 mL)	all-purpose flour
	grated zest of 1 orange and 1 lemon

TOPPING

1 cup (250 mL)	sour cream
1/2 cup (125 mL)	whipping cream
1/4 cup (50 mL)	icing sugar

COULIS

2 packages (10 oz/300 g)	frozen unsweetened raspberries, thawed
	Grand Marnier, to taste
	sugar, to taste

For crust: In a medium bowl, mix together biscuit crumbs, nuts, sugar and cinnamon. Stir in melted butter. Press mixture firmly onto bottom and sides of a greased 8-inch springform pan. Set aside.

For cheesecake: Mix together cream cheese, sugar, eggs, cream and flour, using the lowest speed on an electric mixer, until mixture is thoroughly combined. Stir in the grated orange and lemon zest.

Pour mixture into prepared pan and bake for 10 minutes at 475°F (240°C). Reduce oven temperature to 300°F (150°C) and continue to bake for a further 60 minutes.

For topping: Meanwhile, mix together topping ingredients.

When cake has cooked for 70 minutes, carefully spoon topping over baked cheesecake. Return to oven for another 10 minutes.

Turn oven off and leave cheesecake in oven for 2 to 3 hours. Cover and refrigerate.

For coulis: Sieve thawed raspberries to remove seeds. Add Grand Marnier and sugar to taste. Refrigerate until 1 hour prior to serving, then bring to room temperature.

To assemble: Bring cheesecake to room temperature 2 hours before serving. Pour fruit coulis over cheesecake and serve immediately.

Chèvre Pound Cake

Pound cake is easy to prepare, and the addition of goat's cheese in the cake and the topping gives it a unique bite.

CAKE

1/3 cup (75 mL)	creamy goat's cheese
3	eggs, room temperature
1 tbsp (15 mL)	pure vanilla extract
1 1/2 cups (375 mL)	all-purpose flour
1/2 cup (125 mL)	granulated sugar
1/4 cup (50 mL)	brown sugar
1 tsp (5 mL)	baking powder
1/2 cup (125 mL)	butter, softened

TOPPING

2/3 cup (150 mL)	creamy goat's cheese
2/3 cup (150 mL)	icing sugar

For cake: Beat together cheese, eggs and vanilla until smooth.

In a separate bowl, whisk together flour, granulated sugar, brown sugar and baking powder.

On low speed, beat butter and half the cheese mixture into the flour mixture. Beat the remaining cheese mixture into the flour mixture, in halves.

Pour into a greased and floured 8- x 4-inch (1.5 L) loaf pan and bake on the middle rack at 350°F (180°C) for 35 minutes or until cake springs back to the touch.

For topping: Beat together cheese and icing sugar until smooth and creamy, about 3 to 5 minutes. Drizzle over cooled cake.

Gingered Pound Cake

This spicy cake is best served with warmed preserves.
The strawberry jam in this recipe is lovely, but ginger marmalade
or a favorite berry flavor would work just as well.

2 cups (500 mL)	cake and pastry flour
1 tbsp (15 mL)	ginger
1 tsp (5 mL)	baking powder
1/4 tsp (2 mL)	salt
pinch	freshly ground nutmeg
pinch	cayenne
1/2 cup (125 mL)	butter, softened
1 cup (250 mL)	granulated sugar
5	eggs
2 tsp (10 mL)	pure vanilla extract
2/3 cup (150 mL)	strawberry jam, for topping

Whisk together flour, ginger, baking powder, salt, nutmeg and cayenne, then sift twice.

Cream together butter and sugar until very pale, light and fluffy.

In a separate bowl, lightly mix eggs with vanilla. Slowly beat egg mixture into creamed mixture until smooth and fluffy.

Stir flour mixture into creamed mixture, in thirds.

Pour into a greased and floured 10-cup (2.5 L) bundt pan and bake at 350°F (180°C), on the middle rack, for 35 minutes or until cake springs back to the touch.

Let cool, then invert onto a serving plate.

In a small pan, heat jam and drizzle over top of cake.

Lemon Poppy Seed Cake

Lemon poppy seed cake never seems to lose its appeal. It was a perennial hit during my tenure at The Senator Restaurant in Toronto, and pastry chefs across the country confirm that it remains a great Canadian favorite.

1 cup (250 mL)	butter
1 cup (250 mL)	granulated sugar
2 cups (500 mL)	all-purpose flour
1 tsp (5 mL)	baking powder
1/4 tsp (2 mL)	salt
	zest of 1 lemon
1/4 cup (50 mL)	poppy seeds
5	eggs
1 tsp (5 mL)	lemon extract
1 tsp (5 mL)	pure vanilla extract
1 recipe	basic glaze (see page 7) or cream cheese icing (see page 8)

Cream together butter and sugar until very pale, light and fluffy.

In a separate bowl, stir together flour, baking powder and salt, then sift. Stir in zest and poppy seeds.

Beat eggs into the creamed mixture, one at a time, then beat in lemon extract and vanilla. Stir in flour in thirds and turn into a greased and floured 8 1/2- x 4 1/2-inch (1.5 L) loaf pan.

Bake on the middle rack at 350°F (180°C) for 1 to 1 1/4 hours or until a tester comes out clean.

Cool and ice with basic glaze or cream cheese icing.

Mocha Walnut Cake

Chris Fenton of Windsor, Ontario, found this recipe in the book she keeps of her family favorites. It was a specialty of her grandmother, Dorothy Hines.

1/2 cup (125 mL)	shortening
1 cup (250 mL)	granulated sugar
2 cups (500 mL)	cake and pastry flour
1 tbsp (15 mL)	baking powder
1/4 tsp (1 mL)	salt
1/2 cup (125 mL)	strong brewed coffee
3/4 cup (175 mL)	chopped walnuts
3	egg whites
1 recipe	mocha buttercream (see page 6)

In a medium bowl, cream shortening, then beat in sugar gradually.

In a separate bowl, sift together flour, baking powder and salt, twice.

Mix dry ingredients and coffee into creamed mixture alternately, one-third of the flour mixture and half of the coffee at a time, beginning and ending with dry ingredients. Add walnuts.

In a clean glass or stainless steel bowl, beat egg whites until stiff; fold into mixture.

Turn into a greased 9-inch (2.5 L) square pan and bake on the middle rack at 350°F (180°C) for 35 to 45 minutes.

Cool on a rack and ice with mocha buttercream.

Elderberry Icebox Cake

This personal favorite features berries that once grew wild in the fencerows and alongside roads throughout Ontario. Now you have to search for the small, tart berries, but they're worth the trouble for their complex, herbal flavor. Small slices are called for when serving this intense cake.

CAKE		TOPPING	
1 cup (250 mL)	granulated sugar	3/4 cup (175 mL)	elderberries, fresh or frozen and thawed
1 lb (500 g)	fresh or frozen and thawed elderberries	1/2 cup (125 mL)	granulated sugar
1/4 cup (50 mL)	lemon juice	1 tbsp (15 mL)	butter
1 1/2 envelopes	unflavored gelatin	2 tsp (10 mL)	instant tapioca
2 cups (500 mL)	whipping cream		
3 dozen	ladyfingers (see recipe on page 13) or		
5 dozen	vanilla wafers		

For cake: Using a food processor, process sugar until fine. Add elderberries and lemon juice and puree. Pour one-third of the puree into a saucepan and add gelatin. Let sit for 5 minutes to soften. Bring to a boil, then simmer for 5 minutes. Whisk in remaining elderberry puree and refrigerate until it thickens, no longer than 2 hours.

Whip cream to stiff peaks. Gradually beat in puree.

Place a layer of cookies in the bottom of a parchment-lined 9-inch (2.5 L) springform pan. Pour in one-third of the elderberry mixture. Arrange cookies around the sides of the pan, and place a second layer of cookies gently over the elderberry mixture. Pour in another one-third of the elderberry mixture. Place a final layer of cookies over top and finish with elderberry mixture.

Refrigerate for 4 hours or overnight to set. Unmold from springform just before serving.

For topping: Combine berries with their juice, sugar, butter and tapioca in a saucepan and let sit for 5 minutes. Bring to a boil, then simmer for 5 minutes. Remove from heat and let cool.

Refrigerate until ready to serve, then spoon over cake immediately before serving.

Elderberry Chiffon Cake

I so love elderberries. They may be hard to find, but they're worth the effort.

CAKE

2 1/4 cups (550 mL)	sifted cake and pastry flour
1 1/2 cups (375 mL)	granulated sugar
2 tsp (10 mL)	baking powder
1 tsp (5 mL)	baking soda
1/2 tsp (2 mL)	salt
6	large eggs, separated +
3	egg whites
3/4 cup (175 mL)	elderberry puree
1/2 cup (125 mL)	vegetable oil
1 tsp (5 mL)	pure vanilla extract
1 tsp (5 mL)	cream of tartar

TOPPING

1 cup (250 mL)	fresh elderberries
1/2 cup (125 mL)	granulated sugar
1 tbsp (15 mL)	butter
1 tbsp (15 mL)	instant tapioca
1 cup (250 mL)	whipping cream

For cake: In a large bowl, stir together then sift flour, 1 1/4 cups (300 mL) of sugar, baking powder, baking soda and salt.

In a separate bowl, beat together egg yolks, elderberry puree, vegetable oil and vanilla. Stir flour mixture into yolk mixture.

In a clean glass or stainless steel bowl, whip egg whites with cream of tartar on low speed until they begin to firm. Add remaining 1/4 cup (50 mL) sugar and increase speed to high, continuing to whip until stiff peaks form.

Fold into batter and turn into an ungreased 10-inch (4 L) tube pan with removable bottom. Bake on the middle rack at 325°F (160°C) for 55 minutes or until a tester comes out clean.

Invert pan to cool by balancing the tube of the pan on the neck of a bottle. Once the cake is completely cool, slide a knife between the cake and the sides of the pan, remove the tube portion, then the outer rim.

For topping: Combine berries, sugar, butter and tapioca in a saucepan and let sit for 5 minutes. Bring to a boil, stirring constantly, then simmer for 5 minutes. Let cool, then refrigerate until ready to serve. Whip the cream. Serve cake slices with a dollop of the whipped cream and elderberry topping.

Aunt Helen's Hungarian Walnut Torta

This is a recipe from my dear Aunt Helen, who is still the best baker in the family and an absolute doll; she's one of those aunts whose greeting involves kissing and pinching of cheeks and whose cakes are unforgettable.

CAKE		ICING	
10	eggs separated	3 cups (750 mL)	granulated sugar
1/2 cup +		3 tbsp (50 mL)	flour
2 tbsp (150 mL)	granulated sugar	2	eggs
3/4 cup (175 mL)	crushed walnuts	3/4 cup (175 mL)	milk
6 tbsp (90 mL)	bread crumbs or	1 cup (250 mL)	unsalted butter, softened
1 cup (250 mL)	flour	4 tbsp (60 mL)	icing sugar
1 tsp (5 mL)	pure vanilla extract	1 tsp (5 mL)	pure vanilla extract
	zest of 1/4 lemon		
1/4 tsp (1 mL)	cream of tartar		

For cake: In a stainless steel bowl over hot water, beat egg yolks with sugar until very thick and lemon colored. Remove from heat and fold in walnuts, bread crumbs or flour, then vanilla and zest.

In a clean glass or stainless steel bowl, beat egg whites with cream of tartar on low speed until they begin to foam. Increase speed to high and beat until stiff; fold into batter.

Turn into 2 greased and floured 9-inch (1.5 L) pans.

Bake at 350°F (160°C) for 25 to 30 minutes or until a tester comes out clean. Cool 5 minutes, remove from pans, and place on rack until cooled completely.

For icing: Whisk together sugar, flour and eggs.

In a saucepan, warm milk, then whisk into egg mixture. Return mixture to pot and cook, stirring, until thick. Let cool.

Beat in butter, 1 tbsp (15 mL) at a time, incorporating fully before the next addition. Beat in sugar and vanilla and continue to mix until smooth and spreadable.

Use to fill and frost cooled torte.

Carrot Cake

This very simple carrot cake is a standard in Ontario and across the country. This recipe can also be baked into muffins, but they will bake much more quickly, so check them after 15 minutes.

2 cups (500 mL)	all-purpose flour
1 2/3 cups (400 mL)	granulated sugar
2 tsp (10 mL)	cinnamon
2 tsp (10 mL)	baking soda
1 tsp (5 mL)	salt
4	eggs
1 cup (250 mL)	oil
4 cups (1 L)	grated carrot
1 recipe	cream cheese icing (see page 8)

Combine flour, sugar, cinnamon, baking soda and salt in a large bowl.

In a separate bowl, lightly beat eggs, then whisk in oil gradually. Stir into the dry ingredients until just mixed.

Fold in grated carrot and turn into 2 greased and floured or parchment-lined 8-inch (1.2 L) cake pans.

Bake on the center rack at 350°F (180°C) for 40 to 45 minutes or until a tester comes out clean.

Let cool, then fill and frost with cream cheese icing.

Honey Pumpkin Breakfast Cake

Mary Lou Harrison, owner of Foster's Fine Catering in Port Hope, Ontario, writes:
"This cake was a blue ribbon winner at the 2000 Port Hope Fall Fair.
My three-year-old twin daughters thought this could be breakfast food and,
with a glass of milk, I don't disagree."

3/4 cup (175 mL)	granulated sugar
1/4 cup (50 mL)	canola oil
1/2 cup (125 mL)	liquid honey
1	egg, lightly beaten
1/2 cup (125 mL)	buttermilk
1 can (14 oz/398 mL)	pumpkin puree
	grated zest of 1 orange
1 tsp (5 mL)	pure vanilla extract
2 cups (500 mL)	whole wheat flour
1 cup (250 mL)	all-purpose flour
2 tsp (10 mL)	cinnamon
2 1/2 tsp (12 mL)	baking soda
1 cup (250 mL)	currants

Whisk together sugar, oil and honey. (If you use the same measure for the honey as for the oil, the honey will slide out more easily.) Add egg. Whisk in buttermilk, pumpkin, orange zest and vanilla.

In a separate bowl, combine whole wheat flour, all-purpose flour, cinnamon, baking soda and currants. Stir into pumpkin mixture until just combined.

Pour into a greased 10-inch (4 L) tube pan and bake on the middle rack at 325°F (160°C) for 45 to 50 minutes or until a tester comes out clean.

Let cool on rack, then remove from pan.

Raspberry Breakfast Cake

Raspberry season finds me with my four-year-old son, happily making our way through the rows of raspberries on any of a number of Ontario pick-your-own farms. The next day, he knows what he's having for breakfast.

1/2 cup (125 mL)	unsalted butter
1/2 cup (125 mL)	granulated sugar
2	eggs
1 tsp (5 mL)	pure vanilla extract
2 cups (500 mL)	whole wheat flour
1 tbsp (15 mL)	baking powder
1/2 tsp (2 mL)	salt
3/4 cup (175 mL)	milk
1 cup (250 mL)	raspberries, fresh or frozen and thawed
1/2 cup (125 mL)	coarsely ground almonds
2 tbsp (25 mL)	brown sugar
1/2 tsp (2 mL)	cinnamon
pinch	freshly ground nutmeg

Cream together butter and sugar until light and fluffy. Beat in eggs, one at a time, then vanilla. Sift together flour, baking powder and salt, twice.

Mix dry ingredients and milk into egg mixture alternately, one-third of the flour mixture and half of the milk at a time, beginning and ending with dry ingredients.

Fold in raspberries and almonds and turn into a greased and floured 8-inch (1.2 L) pan. Combine brown sugar, cinnamon and nutmeg and sprinkle over top.

Bake on the middle rack at 350°F (180°C) for 35 minutes or until a tester comes out clean.

Deb's Walnut Mascarpone Coffee Cake

Cooking instructor Debbie Diament was kind enough to test many of my recipes for this book. I thought I'd invent something with her in mind. Sour cream can be substituted for the mascarpone.

FILLING

1/3 cup (75 mL)	packed brown sugar
2 tsp (10 mL)	cinnamon
1/2 tsp (2 mL)	freshly grated nutmeg
1/4 tsp (1 mL)	cloves
1 3/4 cups (425 mL)	walnut pieces, toasted

CAKE

3 cups (750 mL)	all-purpose flour
2 tsp (10 mL)	baking powder
1 tsp (5 mL)	baking soda
1/4 tsp (1 mL)	salt
2 tsp (10 mL)	cinnamon
1/2 tsp (2 mL)	freshly grated nutmeg
1/4 tsp (1 mL)	cloves
3/4 cup (175 mL)	unsalted butter, softened
1 cup (250 mL)	packed brown sugar
3/4 cup (175 mL)	granulated sugar
3	eggs, room temperature
1 tsp (5 mL)	pure vanilla extract
1 cup (250 mL)	sour cream
3/4 cup (175 mL)	mascarpone cheese

For filling: Combine brown sugar, cinnamon, nutmeg, cloves and walnuts and set aside.

For cake: Stir together flour, baking powder, baking soda, salt, cinnamon, nutmeg and cloves, then sift.

In another bowl, cream butter, brown sugar and granulated sugar until the mixture is light and fluffy. Beat in eggs, one at a time, then vanilla.

Stir together sour cream and mascarpone.

Fold dry ingredients and mascarpone mixture into egg mixture alternately, one-third of the flour mixture and half of the mascarpone at a time, beginning and ending with dry ingredients.

Turn into a greased and floured 10-inch (4 L) tube pan in thirds, alternating with filling mixture and ending with batter.

Bake on the middle rack at 350°F (180°C) for 1 hour or until a tester comes out clean.

Cool in pan for 10 minutes, then remove from pan and cool completely.

Ginger Cake

One benefit of writing about food is indulging friends and family with treats. I've never been more popular than while writing this book, as I volunteered to bake everyone's favorite cake. My aunt loves ginger, so I invented this cake to indulge her.

1/2 cup (125 mL)	butter	pinch	salt
1/2 cup (125 mL)	shortening	1/2 cup (125 mL)	milk
1/4 cup (50 mL)	packed brown sugar	1 tsp (5 mL)	pure vanilla extract
1/2 cup (125 mL)	granulated sugar	1 tbsp (15 mL)	minced orange zest
2 cups (500 mL)	all-purpose flour	1/2 cup (125 mL)	chopped walnuts
1 tbsp (15 mL)	ginger	1 tbsp (15 mL)	flour
1 tsp (5 mL)	cinnamon	1/2 cup (125 mL)	ginger marmalade
1 tsp (5 mL)	baking powder	2 tbsp (25 mL)	icing sugar, for garnish
1/2 tsp (2 mL)	baking soda		

Cream butter and shortening together until very light. Add brown sugar and granulated sugar and cream for 3 minutes more.

In a separate bowl, sift flour, ginger, cinnamon, baking powder, baking soda and salt together, twice.

In another bowl, combine milk, vanilla and orange zest.

Fold dry ingredients and milk mixture into egg mixture alternately, one-third of the flour mixture and half of the milk mixture at a time, beginning and ending with dry ingredients. Coat walnuts in flour and fold in.

Pour into a greased and floured 10-cup (2.5 L) bundt pan and bake on the middle rack at 350°F (180°C) for 35 minutes or until a tester comes out clean.

Let cool for 10 minutes, then remove from pan.

When completely cool, spread marmalade over the top of the cake. Dust with icing sugar just before serving.

Walnut Oat Cakes

This recipe for four small cakes is adapted from a version that appeared in my book
Nice Timing: Gourmet Meals in Minutes. It was originally developed by my husband
to re-create a cake I tried on a Waterloo county farm tour.

4	eggs
4 tbsp (60 mL)	brown sugar
4 tbsp (60 mL)	granulated sugar
1/2 cup (125 mL)	milk
2 tbsp (25 mL)	molasses
1 1/2 cups (375 mL)	quick-cooking rolled oats
1/2 cup (125 mL)	walnuts
4 tbsp (60 mL)	maple syrup

In a large bowl, whip together eggs, brown sugar and granulated sugar until frothy. Add milk and molasses. Stir in oats and walnuts.

Pour into 4 buttered 1 1/2 cup (375 mL) ceramic baking dishes and bake on the middle rack at 350°F (180°C) for 20 minutes or until cakes spring back to the touch.

Serve warm with maple syrup drizzled over top.

Eastern Canada Bakes

The evolution of baking in eastern Canada, like the rest of the country, has been driven by immigration, regional fruits, fashion and technology. The eastern provinces were shaped by waves of new faces; Europeans brought their baking traditions, as did the United Empire Loyalists, and now, of course, world cuisine is leaving its mark.

My passion for regional wild berries is always evident, particularly in this chapter, where cakes are baked with wild blueberries, partridgeberries and cloudberries. As always, there is also a nod to tradition, with a boiled-raisin cake known as war cake, johnnycake, fruitcake and dried-apple cake. Jeannie Dunphy is here again, as she is in *Great Canadian Pies* and *Great Canadian Cookies,* with recipes for cakes from her native Newfoundland. This selection of cakes is all warmth, sweetness and comfort, much like the people who bake them.

Wild Blueberry Cake

Wild blueberries are small and wonderfully sweet. Here they are combined with fresh whipped cream to fill a simple light butter cake.

CAKE	
1 1/2 cups (375 mL)	unsalted butter, softened
1 1/2 cups (375 mL)	granulated sugar
4	eggs, room temperature
1 tsp (5 mL)	pure vanilla extract
2 cups (500 mL)	all-purpose flour
2 tsp (10 mL)	baking powder
1/2 tsp (2 mL)	salt
1 cup (250 mL)	ground almonds
2 tbsp (25 mL)	orange liqueur

ASSEMBLY	
2 cups (500 mL)	whipping cream
1/2 cup (125 mL)	granulated sugar
1 1/2 cups (375 mL)	wild blueberries
1 cup (250 mL)	sliced almonds, toasted, for garnish

For cake: Cream butter on high speed until very light. Add sugar and cream until light and fluffy. Beat eggs in one at time, making sure they are fully mixed in after each addition. Beat in vanilla.

Whisk together flour, baking powder and salt; stir into creamed mixture. Fold in ground almonds and liqueur.

Turn into 2 greased and floured 9-inch (1.5 L) cake pans and bake on the middle rack at 350°F (180°C) for 30 to 35 minutes or until a tester comes out clean.

Remove from the oven and cool for 10 minutes; remove from pan. Let cool completely.

To assemble: Whip cream with 1/2 cup (125 mL) sugar, then use half to frost the top of one of the cakes. Cover with 1 cup (250 mL) of blueberries. Place remaining cake on top and frost with remaining whipped cream. Garnish with remaining blueberries and toasted almonds.

Partridgeberry Cake

Partridgeberries are delightfully tart. In Ontario, I buy them frozen at specialty markets, but if you are unable to find them, substitute cranberries.

CAKE

1 cup (250 mL)	unsalted butter, softened
2 cups (500 mL)	granulated sugar
4	eggs, room temperature
3 cups (750 mL)	all-purpose flour
2 tsp (10 mL)	baking powder
1/2 tsp (2 mL)	baking soda
1/2 tsp (2 mL)	salt
1/4 tsp (1 mL)	cloves
1 cup (250 mL)	buttermilk
1 tsp (5 mL)	pure vanilla extract

ASSEMBLY

3/4 cup (175 mL)	partridgeberry jam
1 recipe	pourable chocolate ganache (see page 18)
1 cup (250 mL)	sliced almonds, toasted, for garnish

For cake: Cream butter and sugar until light and fluffy. Beat eggs in one at time, making sure they are fully mixed in after each addition.

Whisk together flour, baking powder, baking soda, salt and cloves.

Mix buttermilk and vanilla. Stir dry ingredients and buttermilk mixture into creamed mixture alternately, one-third of the flour and half the buttermilk at a time, beginning and ending with dry ingredients.

Turn into 2 greased and floured 8-inch (1.2 L) cake pans and bake on the middle rack at 325°F (160°C) for 45 to 50 minutes or until a tester comes out clean.

Let cakes cool for 10 minutes in pans, then remove from pans to cool completely.

To assemble: Spread partridgeberry jam over 1 cake and place second layer on top. Pour warm ganache over cake and garnish with sliced almonds.

Cloudberry Cake

A favorite export from Newfoundland is cloudberry jam. Rarely seen in other parts of Canada, this acidic little berry makes wonderful preserves. Like all wild berries, they are a precious part of a disappearing world.

2	ladyfinger cake rounds (see recipe on page 13)
1 cup (250 mL)	cloudberry jam
1 cup (250 mL)	whipping cream
1/4 cup (50 mL)	granulated sugar
1/4 cup (50 mL)	honey

Spread jam over surface of both cooled rounds.

Whip cream with sugar and spread half on 1 round. Place second round on base and drizzle with honey.

Top with remaining whipped cream.

Blueberry Cake

Jeannie Dunphy features other recipes from her native Newfoundland on her website at www.recipesnf.terrashare.com. This was a favorite of our recipe-testing team.

1/2 cup (125 mL)	shortening
1/4 tsp (1 mL)	salt
1 tsp (5 mL)	pure vanilla extract
1 cup (250 mL)	granulated sugar
2	eggs, separated
1 1/2 cups (375 mL)	sifted flour
1 tsp (5 mL)	baking powder
1 cup (250 mL)	milk
1 1/2 cups (375 mL)	fresh blueberries
1 tbsp (15 mL)	flour
1 tbsp (15 mL)	granulated sugar

Cream shortening, then gradually beat in salt, vanilla and 3/4 cup (175 mL) sugar. Add egg yolks and beat until light and fluffy.

In a separate bowl, stir together flour and baking powder.

Mix dry ingredients and milk into egg mixture alternately, one-third of the flour mixture and half the milk at a time, beginning and ending with dry ingredients.

In a clean glass or stainless steel bowl, beat egg whites at medium speed until they begin to stiffen. Add remaining 1/4 cup (50 mL) of sugar and increase speed to high, beating until whites are very stiff.

Fold beaten egg whites into egg mixture; toss fresh berries in flour and granulated sugar and fold in.

Turn into a greased 8-inch (1.2 L) square pan. Lightly sprinkle top with 1 tbsp (15 mL) sugar.

Bake in a preheated 350°F (180°C) oven for 50 to 60 minutes or until a tester comes out clean.

Blueberry Upside-down Cake

Jeannie Dunphy's simple cake makes the morning that much more tolerable.
Serve for breakfast with steaming hot coffee and the food section of your local paper.

TOPPING		CAKE	
3 tbsp (50 mL)	butter	1 cup (250 mL)	sifted flour
1 cup (250 mL)	packed brown sugar	2 tsp (10 mL)	baking powder
1 3/4 cups (425 mL)	fresh blueberries	1/4 tsp (1 mL)	salt
1/2 tsp (2 mL)	grated lemon zest	3/4 cup (175 mL)	granulated sugar
2 tsp (10 mL)	lemon juice	1 tsp (5 mL)	cinnamon
		1 tsp (5 mL)	cloves
		1/2 cup (125 mL)	butter
		1	egg
		1/2 cup (125 mL)	milk
		1 tsp (5 mL)	pure vanilla extract

For topping: Melt 3 tbsp (50 mL) butter in an 8-inch (1.2 L) square pan. Remove from heat and add brown sugar; blend well. Spread blueberries over the brown sugar mixture and sprinkle with lemon zest and juice.

For cake: Combine sifted flour, baking powder, salt, sugar, cinnamon and cloves.

In a separate bowl, cream 1/2 cup (125 mL) butter. Add sifted flour mixture, egg, milk and vanilla. Stir until flour is dampened and then beat vigorously for 1 minute. Spoon batter over blueberries.

Bake on the middle rack at 350°F (180°C) for 50 to 60 minutes.

Cool cake in pan for 5 minutes and then invert. Serve warm with whipped cream or ice cream.

Johnnycake

Johnnycake was so much a part of early Canadian life that we were referred to as "johnnycake eaters." This one is much like a cornbread. Look for other recipes by Jeannie Dunphy on her website highlighting Newfoundland cuisine at www.recipesnf.terrashare.com.

1 cup (250 mL)	flour
2 tsp (10 mL)	baking powder
1/4 tsp (1 mL)	salt
1 cup (250 mL)	cornmeal
1/4 cup (50 mL)	granulated sugar
	butter size of an egg (3 tbsp/50 mL)
1	egg, well-beaten
1 cup (250 mL)	milk

Sift flour, baking powder and salt together. Add cornmeal and sugar.

Melt butter and add to well-beaten egg and milk. Add to dry ingredients and beat lightly.

Turn into a greased 9-inch (23 cm) pie plate and bake on the middle rack at 350°F (180°C) for 30 to 40 minutes or until lightly browned around the edges.

Serve warm with butter.

Light Fruitcake

Jeannie Dunphy's home-style Newfoundland fruitcake can be baked in a
springform pan or in a round tin. It keeps well and can be frozen for months.
Lemon zest can be used rather than extract.

1 cup (250 mL)	butter
1 1/2 cups (375 mL)	granulated sugar
5	eggs, separated
3 cups (750 mL)	sifted all-purpose flour
1 tsp (5 mL)	baking powder
1/4 tsp (1 mL)	salt
1 cup (250 mL)	milk
1 tsp (5 mL)	lemon extract
1/2 cup (125 mL)	blanched almonds
2 cups (500 mL)	mixed peel
1 1/2 cups (375 mL)	candied cherries
1 cup (250 mL)	light sultana raisins

Cream butter and sugar until very light and fluffy. Beat in well-beaten egg yolks.

In a separate bowl, sift together 2 1/2 cups (625 mL) flour, baking powder and salt.

Combine milk and lemon extract.

Mix dry ingredients and milk into egg mixture alternately, one-third of the flour mixture and half the milk at a time, beginning and ending with dry ingredients.

Toss dried fruit and nuts in remaining 1/2 cup (125 mL) flour and fold into the batter.

In a clean glass or stainless steel bowl, beat egg whites on low speed until they begin to foam. Increase speed to high and beat until stiff but not dry. Fold into the cake.

Turn into a greased, parchment-lined 9-inch (1.5 L) cake pan.

Bake on the middle rack at 325°F (160°C) for 2 1/2 to 3 hours or until a tester comes out clean.

Partridgeberry Spice Cake

Jeannie Dunphy passionately promotes her native Newfoundland cuisine. I have been pleased to find sources for frozen partridgeberries at specialty fruit markets in Ontario, so I can bake her terrific spice cake at home. If partridgeberries are unavailable to you, cranberries make an excellent substitute.

1 cup (250 mL)	shortening
1 cup (250 mL)	granulated sugar
1	egg, beaten
1 cup (250 mL)	raisins
1/2 cup (125 mL)	chopped nuts
1 3/4 cups (425 mL)	flour
1/4 tsp (1 mL)	salt
1 tsp (5 mL)	baking soda
1 tsp (5 mL)	baking powder
1 tsp (5 mL)	cinnamon
1/2 tsp (2 mL)	cloves
1/2 cup (125 mL)	water
1 cup (250 mL)	partridgeberries

Cream together shortening and sugar until light and fluffy. Beat in egg; stir in raisins and nuts.

In a separate bowl, whisk together flour, salt, baking soda, baking powder, cinnamon and cloves, then sift.

In thirds, stir flour mixture gently into creamed mixture. Gently stir in water, then fold in berries.

Turn into a greased 10-inch (4 L) tube pan and bake on the middle rack at 350°F (180°C) for 1 hour or until a tester comes out clean.

Grandma Rockey's War Cake

This recipe is excerpted from my first book, Recipes for Homemade Love. Grandma Rockey was a strong, no-nonsense woman born in 1890 who raised 10 kids and 40 grandchildren. Seven of the children were born in Wales, before the Rockey clan packed their bags and set sail for Nova Scotia just before the Great Depression. This recipe comes from a time when fruit was hard to obtain and raisins were often the only thing available. It became known as a war cake and was so popular that it remains a family tradition. Figs, prunes or nuts can be added if you want to fancy it up.

2 cups (500 mL)	seedless raisins
1 cup (250 mL)	brown sugar
1 cup (250 mL)	hot water
1/2 cup (125 mL)	unsalted butter
1/2 tsp (2 mL)	salt
1/4 tsp (1 mL)	cinnamon
1/2 tsp (2 mL)	freshly grated nutmeg
1/2 tsp (2 mL)	cloves
2 cups (500 mL)	sifted flour
1 tsp (5 mL)	baking soda
1 tsp (5 mL)	pure vanilla extract

Place raisins, sugar, hot water, butter, salt, cinnamon, nutmeg and cloves in large saucepan and bring to boil. Reduce heat and simmer for 10 minutes. Set aside to cool until lukewarm.

Sift in flour and baking soda, then add vanilla. Turn into a well-greased 9-inch (1.5 L) pan and bake on the middle rack at 325°F (160°C) for 1 1/2 to 2 hours or until a tester comes out clean.

Raisin Apple Cake

Slicing and drying fresh apples was just one of the ways thrifty bakers made the brutal eastern winter tolerable in earlier times. The recipes continue to be made, often using store-bought dried apples, because their taste is sensational. The winters are still brutal. Warming the maple syrup is a nice touch.

3/4 cup (175 mL)	raisins		1/4 tsp (1 mL)	salt
3/4 cup (175 mL)	dried apple slices		1 tsp (5 mL)	cinnamon
1/3 cup (175 mL)	rum		1/2 tsp (2 mL)	freshly grated nutmeg
3/4 cup (175 mL)	chopped walnuts		2 cups (500 mL)	golden brown sugar
1 tbsp (15 mL)	flour		1/2 cup (125 mL)	granulated sugar
2 cups (500 mL)	all-purpose flour		3	eggs
2 tsp (10 mL)	baking powder		1 cup (250 mL)	canola oil
1 tsp (5 mL)	baking soda		1/2 cup (125 mL)	maple syrup

In a medium bowl, soak raisins and apples in rum for 1 hour or until soft. Toss nuts in 1 tbsp (15 ml) flour.

Meanwhile, in a separate bowl, whisk together all-purpose flour, baking powder, baking soda, salt, cinnamon and nutmeg.

Using another bowl, beat brown sugar, granulated sugar and eggs until light and thick, about 5 minutes. Gently mix in oil, then fold in fruit and nuts.

Turn into a parchment-lined greased 13- x 9-inch (3.5 L) pan and bake on the middle rack at 325°F (160°C) for 1 hour and 15 minutes or until a tester comes out clean.

Drizzle maple syrup over when ready to serve.

Far Breton

Is it a flan, a pudding, a bread or a thin cake? However you choose to categorize this prune-filled classic, serve it to warm body and soul on a blustery day.

1 cup (250 mL)	pitted prunes
1/4 cup (50 mL)	dark rum
3 tbsp (50 mL)	unsalted butter, softened
3	large eggs
1 1/4 cups (300 mL)	milk
1	vanilla bean
1/2 cup (125 mL)	all-purpose flour
1/2 cup (125 mL)	granulated sugar
2 tbsp (25 mL)	icing sugar, for garnish

Soak prunes in rum and cover with plastic wrap; let sit for 1 hour.

Meanwhile, using a food processor, pulse butter and eggs.

In a small pan, warm milk with vanilla bean to infuse. Remove bean and discard.

Add milk to egg mixture and pulse.

Add flour and granulated sugar and pulse until combined.

Turn batter into buttered 8-cup (2 L) ceramic dish and bake on the middle rack at 425°F (220°C) for 10 minutes or until edges puff up. Reduce heat to 350°F (180°C) and bake for 35 to 40 minutes or until puffed and set.

Serve warm, dusted with icing sugar.

Western Canada Bakes

There is so much to love about the western provinces: big skies, endless prairies, majestic mountains and grand forests. And cake. Marvelous cakes, baked in farm kitchens, resort ovens and apartments with an ocean view. Baking has never waned in popularity here; it has always been an intrinsic part of western hospitality.

Old favorites, from a simple spice cake to matrimonial cake and gingerbread, are here. Saskatoon berries are essential to Prairie baking, and here we showcase them in a cake and sensational muffins. Icelandic vinarterta is a prime example of the Canadian national tendency to take a heritage cake and, over generations, make it our own. There's also a salute to Vancouver's obsession with coffee in a java-inspired chocolate espresso torte. The flavors in these recipes reflect the diversity of this enormous region but, whatever your taste, you will find something here to satisfy your sweet tooth.

Saskatoon Berry Muffins

Saskatoon berries are small, sweet berries that are traditionally baked into pies and made into jam in western provinces. They are sometimes available frozen in specialty stores in other parts of Canada. These muffins are wonderful served warm from the oven.

1/2 cup (125 mL)	unsalted butter, softened
1 cup (250 mL)	granulated sugar
2	eggs
1 tsp (5 mL)	pure vanilla extract
2 cups (500 mL)	all-purpose flour
1 tsp (5 mL)	baking soda
1/2 tsp (2 mL)	baking powder
1/2 tsp (2 mL)	salt
1 cup (250 mL)	buttermilk
1 cup (250 mL)	saskatoon berries, fresh or frozen and thawed

Cream together butter and sugar until light and fluffy. Beat in eggs, one at a time, then vanilla.

In a separate bowl, combine flour, baking soda, baking powder and salt.

Mix dry ingredients and buttermilk into egg mixture alternately, one-third of the flour mixture and half of the buttermilk at a time, beginning and ending with dry ingredients. Fold in saskatoon berries.

Spoon into a greased or lined muffin tin and bake on the middle rack at 350°F (180°C) for 15 minutes or until a tester comes out clean.

Saskatoon Berry Coffee Cake

Wild blueberries are an excellent substitute for saskatoon berries.

1/3 cup (75 mL)	sliced almonds
1/3 cup (75 mL)	brown sugar
1 tsp (5 mL)	cinnamon
1 1/2 cups (375 mL)	all-purpose flour
1/2 cup (125 mL)	granulated sugar
1 tbsp (15 mL)	baking powder
1 tsp (5 mL)	ginger
1/4 tsp (1 mL)	salt
1/2 cup (125 mL)	cold butter, cubed
1	egg
2/3 cup (150 mL)	sour cream
1 tsp (5 mL)	pure vanilla extract
1 cup (250 mL)	saskatoon berries, fresh or frozen and thawed
1/4 cup (50 mL)	maple syrup

Combine almonds, brown sugar and cinnamon and crumble into the bottom of a greased 8- x 4-inch (1.5 L) loaf pan.

In a large bowl, whisk together flour, sugar, baking powder, ginger and salt. Cut in butter until mixture comprises coarse, pea-sized crumbs.

In a separate bowl, combine egg, sour cream and vanilla. Stir into flour mixture.

Fold in saskatoon berries.

Turn into loaf pan and bake on the middle rack at 350°F (180°C) for 1 hour or until a tester comes out clean.

Serve slices warm or cool with maple syrup drizzled over.

Tomato Soup Cake with Barley Flour

This variation on a cake with real kitsch appeal was developed by
The Alberta Barley Commission for its website, www.albertabarley.com.

1 cup (250 mL)	granulated sugar
1/2 cup (125 mL)	shortening
1 can (10 oz/284 mL)	condensed tomato soup
1 tbsp (15 mL)	water
1 cup (250 mL)	whole barley flour
1/2 cup (125 mL)	all-purpose flour
1 tsp (5 mL)	baking soda
1 tsp (5 mL)	cinnamon
1/2 tsp (2 mL)	salt
1/2 tsp (2 mL)	cloves
1 cup (250 mL)	raisins
1 recipe	cream cheese icing (see page 8)

Cream together the sugar, shortening, condensed soup and water.

In a separate bowl, mix barley and all-purpose flours, baking soda, cinnamon, salt and cloves, then beat into the soup mixture. Add raisins and stir well.

Spread batter in a greased 8-inch (2 L) square pan.

Bake on the middle rack at 350°F (180°C) for 35 to 40 minutes or until a tester comes out clean.

Remove from oven and cool on a rack.

When cool, top with cream cheese icing.

Vinarterta

Historian Jim Anderson of Manitoba has extensively researched this Icelandic layered coffee cake, which has been adopted by Prairie bakers. This cake's popularity may have stemmed from the fact that the thin cake layers had a fair chance of success in early, rustic ovens.

Prune filling (Sveskjumauk á vínartertu) is popular for Prairie vinarterta, but can be replaced with rhubarb jam. The prune filling recipe is adapted from one sent to Jim Anderson by Nanna Rögnvaldardóttir.

CAKE

1 cup (250 mL)	butter, softened
1 cup (250 mL)	granulated sugar
2	eggs
1 tsp (5 mL)	pure vanilla extract
4 cups (1 L)	all-purpose flour
1 tbsp (15 mL)	baking powder
1 tsp (5 mL)	cardamom
1/4 tsp (1 mL)	salt
1/2 cup (125 mL)	milk

PRUNE FILLING

1 1/4 cups (300 mL)	pitted prunes
1 1/4 cups (300 mL)	granulated sugar
1 tbsp (15 mL)	cinnamon
1/2 tsp (2 mL)	cloves
1/2 tsp (2 mL)	cardamom

For cake: Cream butter, then beat in sugar until light and fluffy. Beat in eggs, one at a time, whisking well between additions. Add vanilla.

In a separate bowl, combine flour, baking powder, cardamom and salt.

Mix dry ingredients and milk into egg mixture alternately, one-third of the flour mixture and half the milk at a time, beginning and ending with dry ingredients. Knead the dough lightly until smooth; it should be soft. Divide the dough into 6 equal parts, cover with plastic wrap and refrigerate for 1 hour.

On a floured work surface, roll each part out into a thin 9-inch (23 cm) disc. Arrange the circles on parchment-lined baking sheets and bake on the middle rack at 375°F (190°C) for 12 minutes, or until beginning to brown at the edges. Let cool.

For prune filling: In a small saucepan, combine prunes, sugar, cinnamon, cloves and cardamom and cover with 1 cup (250 mL) water.

Bring to a boil then simmer, stirring often, until the prunes are soft and the syrup has thickened, approximately 20 to 30 minutes.

Let cool slightly, then pulse in a food processor until smooth.

To assemble: Stack the layers with the prune filling or jam between.

Wrap in foil, and keep for at least a couple of days. If stored in a cool place, the cake will keep for weeks and improve with age.

Chocolate Espresso Torte

Espresso bars dotted the Vancouver landscape long before the coffee explosion hit the rest of Canada. This cake is a coffee lover's dream.

MERINGUES

8	egg whites
1/4 tsp (1 mL)	cream of tartar
pinch	salt
1 tsp (5 mL)	pure vanilla extract
1 1/2 cups (375 mL)	fruit sugar or granulated sugar processed in a blender until fine

ASSEMBLY

1 cup (250 mL)	mocha buttercream (see recipe on page 6)
2 cups (500 mL)	whipping cream
1/4 cup (50 mL)	coffee liqueur
1 cup (250 mL)	chocolate-covered espresso beans, for garnish

For meringues: Cover 2 baking sheets with parchment. On paper, draw three 9-inch (23 cm) circles.

In a clean glass or stainless steel bowl, beat egg whites until frothy. Beat in cream of tartar, salt and vanilla until soft peaks form. Very gradually beat in sugar until stiff peaks form. Spoon mixture onto circles, smoothing tops.

Bake at 250°F (120°C) for 1 hour. Turn off heat and let meringues cool in oven for at least 6 hours or overnight. Carefully peel paper from meringues.

To assemble: Spread mocha buttercream over 2 meringue layers.

In a large bowl, whip cream; beat in coffee liqueur.

Place 1 buttercream-covered meringue on serving plate and spread with one-third of the cream. Top with plain meringue, then half of the remaining cream. Place second buttercream-covered layer on top; spread with remaining cream. Garnish with coffee beans. Cover loosely and chill for 24 hours before serving.

Dream Cake

Lorraine Stevenson of The Manitoba Co-operator newspaper has been a wonderful resource for Prairie recipes. This recipe from the staff at the Co-operator appears in their book Kitchen Culture: Recipes from the 40s, 50s and 60s. Apparently it was "a must in just about every household" in the fabulous 40s.

CAKE

1 cup (250 mL)	flour
1/2 cup (125 mL)	butter
1 tbsp (15 mL)	granulated sugar

TOPPING

1 cup (250 mL)	chopped walnuts
1 cup (250 mL)	coconut
1/3 cup (75 mL)	brown sugar
2 tbsp (25 mL)	flour
1/2 tsp (2 mL)	baking powder
1/2 tsp (2 mL)	pure vanilla extract
2	eggs

For cake: Rub flour, butter and sugar together and press into an 8-inch (1.2 L) pan.

Bake on the middle rack at 300°F (150°C) until pale brown.

For topping: Mix walnuts, coconut, brown sugar, flour, baking powder, vanilla and eggs until well blended. Spread on the lightly browned shortbread base and return to the oven. Bake for an additional 30 minutes.

Cool thoroughly before cutting.

Honey Chocolate Cake

*The Manitoba Co-operator's book, Kitchen Culture: Recipes from the 40s, 50s and 60s,
features several cakes from the 1950s—standards such as upside-down cake,
spice cake, jam cake and this yummy honey cake.*

CAKE	
1/2 cup (125 mL)	shortening
2 cups (500 mL)	sifted cake and pastry flour
1 1/2 tsp (7 mL)	baking soda
1 tsp (5 mL)	salt
2/3 cup (150 mL)	water
1 1/4 cups (300 mL)	honey
2	eggs, unbeaten
2 1/2 squares	unsweetened chocolate, melted
1 tsp (5 mL)	pure vanilla extract

FROSTING	
1	egg white
dash	salt
1/2 cup (125 mL)	honey

For cake: Mix shortening just to soften. Sift in flour, baking soda and salt.

Combine water and honey and add 1/2 cup (125 mL) of this liquid mixture, with the eggs, to the flour mixture. Mix until all flour is dampened; then beat 1 minute.

Add remaining honey mixture, melted chocolate, and vanilla. Blend by hand or mixer at slow speed for 2 minutes longer. (Count only actual beating time or count strokes. Allow about 150 full strokes per minute. Scrape bowl and spoon or beater often.) Batter will be thin.

Pour batter into 2 greased and floured 9-inch (1.5 L) pans.

Bake on the middle rack at 350°F (180°C) for 30 minutes or until a tester comes out clean.

For frosting: Beat egg white with salt until stiff but not dry. Continue to beat, while adding honey in fine stream, until frosting holds its shape. Frosting should be consumed the same day.

Totin' Cake

Lorraine Stevenson of The Manitoba Co-operator suggests that this cake may have received its name because it is suitable for totin' around. It comes from The Manitoba Co-operator's book, Kitchen Culture: Recipes from the 40s, 50s and 60s.

TOPPING

1/2 cup (125 mL)	firmly packed brown sugar
1/2 cup (125 mL)	chopped walnuts or pecans

CAKE

2 1/4 cups (550 mL)	sifted all-purpose flour
1 tbsp + 1/2 tsp (17 mL)	baking powder
1/2 tsp (2 mL)	salt
1/2 cup (125 mL)	butter
1 1/3 cups (325 mL)	firmly packed brown sugar
2	eggs
1 cup (250 mL)	milk
1 tsp (5 mL)	pure vanilla extract
1 cup (250 mL)	miniature marshmallows

For topping: In a large bowl, combine brown sugar with nuts; reserve.

For cake: In a separate bowl, combine flour, baking powder and salt.

In a third bowl, cream together butter and brown sugar until fluffy. Add eggs, one at a time, beating well after each.

Combine milk and vanilla. Mix with dry ingredients into egg mixture alternately, one-third of the flour mixture and half the milk mixture at a time, beginning and ending with dry ingredients.

Arrange marshmallows in the bottom of a greased and floured 9-inch (2.5 L) cake pan, to within 1/2 inch (1 cm) of the sides. Sprinkle nut mixture on top of marshmallows, and pour batter into pan.

Bake on the middle rack at 350°F (180°C) for 40 to 45 minutes or until tester comes out clean. Be careful not to puncture marshmallow layer.

Cool in pan on wire rack, then remove from pan.

Matrimonial Cake

To the rest of Canada, this recipe is known as date squares, but in the west it has always been matrimonial cake.

FILLING

3 cups (750 mL)	chopped dates
3/4 cup (175 mL)	water
3 tbsp (50 mL)	brown sugar
	zest of 1/2 lemon
1/4 cup (50 mL)	lemon juice

BARS

1 1/2 cups (375 mL)	all-purpose flour
1 1/2 cups (375 mL)	rolled oats
1 cup (250 mL)	lightly packed brown sugar
1/2 tsp (2 mL)	baking soda
1/2 tsp (2 mL)	salt
1 cup (250 mL)	unsalted butter, softened

For filling: Combine dates, water, 3 tbsp (50 mL) brown sugar, zest and juice in a medium-sized heavy-bottomed saucepan. Bring to a boil; reduce heat to simmer and cook until dates are soft, about 10 minutes. Stir often. Transfer to a shallow dish and place in refrigerator to cool.

For bars: In a separate bowl, combine flour, oats, brown sugar, baking soda and salt. Rub in butter until mixture resembles coarse crumbs. Press half the dough into the bottom of a greased 9-inch (2.5 L) pan. Cover with cooled date filling and top with remaining dough.

Bake at 350°F (180°C) for 35 to 40 minutes or until lightly browned on top.

Makes 16 bars.

Spice Cake

Spice cakes have always been popular in the west, and there are almost as many recipes as there are bakers. This recipe is adapted from one I found in an old Five Roses Flour cookbook.

1 cup (250 mL)	butter, softened
1 1/2 cups (375 mL)	granulated sugar
3	eggs
3 cups (750 mL)	all-purpose flour
1 tsp (5 mL)	baking powder
1/2 tsp (2 mL)	baking soda
1 tsp (5 mL)	freshly ground nutmeg
1 tsp (5 mL)	cinnamon
1/4 tsp (1 mL)	cloves
1 cup (250 mL)	buttermilk
1 cup (250 mL)	raisins
1 tbsp (15 mL)	flour
1 cup (250 mL)	chopped walnuts

Cream butter until light. Beat in sugar until very light. Beat in eggs, one at a time.

In a separate bowl, combine flour, baking powder, baking soda, nutmeg, cinnamon and cloves.

Mix dry ingredients and buttermilk into egg mixture alternately, one-third of the flour mixture and half the buttermilk at a time, beginning and ending with dry ingredients. Toss raisins in flour and fold in along with walnuts.

Turn batter into a greased and floured 10-inch (4 L) tube pan. Bake on the middle rack at 350°F (180°C) for 1 hour or until a tester comes out clean.

Gingerbread Cake

This gingerbread cake is light and moist and likely warmed pioneer spirits on cold Prairie nights. Unsulfured molasses has a cleaner, better taste because it is made from pure cane juice.

1/2 cup (125 mL)	butter
1/2 cup (125 mL)	water
1/2 cup (125 mL)	molasses
1/2 cup (125 mL)	brown sugar
1	egg
1/4 cup (50 mL)	grated fresh ginger
1 1/2 cups (375 mL)	all-purpose flour
1 tsp (5 mL)	baking soda
1 tsp (5 mL)	cinnamon
1/4 tsp (1 mL)	freshly ground nutmeg
1/4 tsp (1 mL)	salt

Melt butter, water, molasses and brown sugar in a medium saucepan over low heat. Cool, then beat in egg and stir in ginger.

In a bowl, combine flour, baking soda, cinnamon, nutmeg and salt; fold into moist ingredients.

Turn into a greased and floured 9-inch (2.5 L) cake pan and bake on the middle rack at 350°F (180°C) for 30 minutes or until a tester comes out clean.

Cool before serving.

Almond Bundt Cake

This cake suits both a bustling Vancouver espresso bar or a warm Prairie kitchen.
Either way, serve warm with plenty of steaming hot coffee.

1 1/2 cups (375 mL)	sliced almonds		1 tsp (5 mL)	baking powder
1/2 cup (125 mL)	unsalted butter, room temperature		1/4 tsp (1 mL)	salt
1 cup (250 mL)	granulated sugar		1 cup (250 mL)	sour cream
2	eggs		3/4 cup (175 mL)	almond paste
1 tsp (5 mL)	pure vanilla extract		1/2 cup (125 mL)	whipping cream
2 cups (500 mL)	all-purpose flour		1/4 cup (50 mL)	almond liqueur
1 tsp (5 mL)	baking soda		4 tbsp (60 mL)	milk
			4 tbsp (60 mL)	icing sugar

Toast almonds on a baking sheet at 300°F (150°C) until golden and fragrant, 3 to 4 minutes.

In a large bowl, cream together butter and sugar until light and fluffy. Beat in eggs, one at a time, followed by vanilla. In a separate bowl, sift together flour, baking soda, baking powder and salt, twice.

Mix dry ingredients and sour cream into egg mixture alternately, one-third of the flour mixture and half the sour cream at a time, beginning and ending with dry ingredients. Stir in 1 1/4 cups (300 mL) almonds.

Knead almond paste until soft, then combine in food processor with whipping cream and almond liqueur. Transfer half the cake batter into a greased and floured 10-inch (2.5 L) bundt pan. Layer with half the almond mixture, then remaining batter. Add milk and icing sugar to remaining almond mixture and pour over cake.

Bake on the middle rack at 350°F (180°C) for 30 minutes. Remove from oven and sprinkle remaining toasted almonds over the top. Return to oven for an additional 30 minutes or until a tester comes out clean.

Honey Barley Chiffon Cake

Miriam Schnee of Gwynne, Alberta, offers this chiffon cake recipe, which I found on the Alberta Barley Commission's website. Miriam writes, "This recipe is softer and moister than any chiffon cake made with sugar and wheat flour that I've tasted."

6	eggs, separated
1/2 tsp (2 mL)	cream of tartar
3/4 cup (175 mL)	honey
3/4 cup (175 mL)	water
1/2 cup (125 mL)	oil
1 1/2 cups (375 mL)	whole barley flour
2 1/2 tsp (12 mL)	baking powder

In a clean glass or stainless steel bowl, whip egg whites and cream of tartar until very stiff. Add 1/4 cup (50 mL) of honey and whip until combined. Set aside.

Put egg yolks, remaining 1/2 cup (125 mL) of honey, water, oil, barley flour and baking powder in a blender and blend at high speed until pale.

Gently fold blender mixture into the egg whites and turn into an ungreased 16-cup (4 L) angel food pan.

Bake on the middle rack at 350°F (180°C) for 60 to 65 minutes or until cakes springs back. Leave cake in pan and invert to cool.

Heritage Cakes

Although the origins of cake can be traced to the second century BCE, cake baking in Canada most interests me. What did the pioneers bake on their trek across the country, what did early farmers eat in the prairie fields and what was baked in wood stoves across the country? How did immigration, technology and fashion mold our tastes, and how does my great-great-grandmother's baking compare to my own?

Well, the similarities are astounding. Cakes have figured prominently on our tables from the time we carved that table out of the forest. There is little here that you won't recognize: soft gingerbread, pound cake, jelly rolls and, of course, chocolate cake. Canadian heritage cakes could fill several cookbooks and they need little alteration to come out moist and delicious. For more information on the baking of times past, see "The History of Cake."

Common Gingerbread

Recipes for soft gingerbread or cake appear in cookbooks from every era. This recipe appeared in Catherine Parr Traill's Canadian Settler's Guide *from 1855: "Treacle 1 1/2 lb: seconds flour 2 lb: butter 2 oz: ginger 1 oz: spices 2 oz: of pearl-ash one dessert-spoonful; mix with milk warmed, into a dough, let it stand till it rises, bake on tins, and cut in squares." This was a time when it was assumed that everyone knew how to bake a cake, or cook a roast for that matter. Later food writers would provide extra help, as in this recipe, inspired by an early Five Roses Flour cookbook.*

2 tbsp (25 mL)	butter
1/2 cup (125 mL)	molasses
1/2 cup (125 mL)	brown sugar
1/2 cup (125 mL)	buttermilk
1	egg
1 1/2 cups (375 mL)	all-purpose flour
2 tsp (10 mL)	baking soda
1 tsp (5 mL)	ginger
1/4 tsp (1 mL)	mace
1/4 tsp (1 mL)	salt

Combine butter, molasses, brown sugar and buttermilk in a medium saucepan over low heat. Heat until butter is melted and remove from heat. When cool, beat in egg.

In a bowl, combine flour, baking soda, ginger, mace and salt; fold into moist ingredients.

Turn into a greased and floured 9-inch (1.5 L) cake pan and bake in the middle of a preheated 350°F (180°C) oven for 30 minutes or until a tester comes out clean.

Cool before serving.

Muskoka Chocolate Cake

This recipe was inspired by one sent to me by Mary Williamson of the Culinary Historians of Ontario. Her original was contributed by Rena Winter to a book called Recipes Compiled and Arranged by the Ladies' Aid Society of Broadway Tabernacle, Toronto.

CAKE	
3/4 cup (175 mL)	cocoa (undutched)
1 cup (250 mL)	milk
1	egg +
2	yolks
2 cups (500 mL)	sifted all-purpose flour
1 cup (250 mL)	granulated sugar
1 1/2 tsp (7 mL)	baking soda
1/4 tsp (1 mL)	salt
3 tbsp (50 mL)	unsalted butter

FROSTING	
2 cups (500 mL)	granulated sugar
1/2 cup (125 mL)	water
2	egg whites
pinch	cream of tartar
1/2 tsp (2 mL)	pure vanilla extract

For cake: In a medium bowl, whisk together cocoa, 1/2 cup (125 mL) milk, egg and yolks.

In a separate bowl, whisk together flour, sugar, baking soda and salt.

In a heavy-bottomed pot over low heat, cook cocoa mixture, stirring constantly until the first bubble appears. Remove from heat and add remaining milk and butter; stir. Stir in dry ingredients.

Pour into 2 greased 9-inch (1.5 L) cake pans and bake on the middle rack at 350°F (180°C) for 45 to 55 minutes or until a tester comes out clean.

Let cool for 10 minutes then remove from cake pans.

For frosting: In a heavy-bottomed pan over high heat, cook sugar with water until fine strands fall from a fork lifted out of the syrup (230°F/110°C).

Meanwhile, in a clean glass or stainless steel bowl, beat egg whites with cream of tartar until stiff. Slowly pour hot syrup into egg whites, beating constantly. Beat in vanilla.

Frost cake immediately. As soon as this topping begins to set, it hardens and cannot be worked without becoming grainy.

Valentine Cake

Mary Williamson of the Culinary Historians of Ontario writes, "I have my aunt's recipe for a valentine cake, which as a child I always looked forward to. My mother mentions it in a letter written in the early 1940s. The recipe comes from Emily G. Williamson (1880-1957)."

1/2 cup (125 mL)	butter
1 cup (250 mL)	granulated sugar
2	eggs
1 tsp (5 mL)	pure vanilla extract
2 1/2 cups (625 mL)	flour
1/4 tsp (1 mL)	salt
2 tsp (10 mL)	baking powder
3/4 cup (175 mL)	milk
1 cup (250 mL)	gumdrops, finely chopped
1 cup (250 mL)	raisins

In a large bowl, cream together butter and sugar until light and fluffy. Beat in eggs, one at a time, and vanilla.

In a separate bowl, stir then sift together 2 cups (500 mL) flour, salt and baking powder.

Mix dry ingredients and milk into creamed mixture alternately, one-third of the flour mixture and half the milk at a time, beginning and ending with dry ingredients.

Toss gumdrops and raisins in remaining 1/2 cup (125 mL) flour and fold into batter.

Turn into a greased 9-inch (1.5 L) cake tin and bake on the middle rack at 300°F (150°C) for 1 1/4 to 1 1/2 hours or until cake springs back to the touch.

Jelly Roll

This jelly roll comes from a wonderful handmade family cookbook compiled by my friend Keith's Aunt Ruby, which is aptly called Aunt Ruby's Recipes. *She wrote the book in memory of her sister, Mabel, who shared these recipes with her at home on the farm. Jelly roll was a favorite in the fabulous 50s.*

3	eggs, separated
1 cup (250 mL)	granulated sugar
2 tbsp (25 mL)	condensed milk
1 cup (250 mL)	all-purpose flour
2 tsp (10 mL)	baking powder
1/4 tsp (1 mL)	salt
1/2 tsp (2 mL)	lemon extract
1/4 cup (50 mL) (approx.)	granulated sugar
3/4 cup (175 mL)	jam or lemon filling

Beat egg yolks with sugar and milk.

In a clean glass or stainless steel bowl, beat egg whites until stiff, then fold into the yolk mixture.

Stir and sift together flour, baking powder and salt and add to creamed mixture. Stir in lemon extract.

Pour into a parchment-lined 15- x 10-inch (2 L) jelly roll pan.

Bake in the middle of a preheated 350°F (180°C) oven for 15 to 20 minutes or until cake springs back to the touch.

Spread out a damp towel and dust with approximately 1/4 cup (50 mL) granulated sugar. Turn the hot jelly roll onto the towel, peel off parchment, and roll up lengthwise. Let cool.

Before serving, spread with jam or lemon filling and roll again.

Crazy Cake

Here's another classic from Aunt Ruby (see preceding page). I remember my own grandmother making crazy cake—and tomato soup cake for that matter—but her recipe didn't make it into the archives. I imagine it looked a lot like this.

1/2 cup (125 mL)	All-Bran cereal
1 cup (250 mL)	cold coffee
1/4 cup (50 mL)	vegetable oil
1 tbsp (15 mL)	vinegar
1 tsp (5 mL)	pure vanilla extract
1 1/4 cups (300 mL)	all-purpose flour
1 cup (250 mL)	granulated sugar
1/4 cup (50 mL)	cocoa, undutched
1 tsp (5 mL)	cinnamon
1 tsp (5 mL)	baking soda
1/2 tsp (2 mL)	salt

In a large bowl, combine cereal with coffee and let stand until cereal is moist. Stir in vegetable oil, vinegar and vanilla.

In a separate bowl, whisk together flour, sugar, cocoa, cinnamon, baking soda and salt. Stir into moist ingredients.

Turn into a greased 8-inch (2 L) square pan and bake on the middle rack at 350°F (180°C) for 35 minutes.

All-in-One Cake

This cake from Aunt Ruby's Recipes (see page 101) was attributed to
Nellie Nighswander and dated 1976. A similar recipe could be found in
many cookbooks from the mid-1950s on.

1/2 cup (125 mL)	butter, softened
1 cup (250 mL)	granulated sugar
3	eggs, separated
1 cup (250 mL)	all-purpose flour
1 tsp (5 mL)	baking powder
4 tbsp (60 mL)	milk
1/4 tsp (1 mL)	cream of tartar
1 cup (250 mL)	shredded coconut

In a large bowl, cream together butter and 1/2 cup (125 mL) sugar until very light and fluffy. Beat in egg yolks one at a time.

Combine flour and baking powder. Mix dry ingredients and milk into butter mixture alternately, one-third of the flour mixture and half the milk at a time, beginning and ending with dry ingredients.

Turn into a greased 8-inch (2 L) square pan.

In a clean glass or stainless steel bowl, beat egg whites with cream of tartar on low speed until they begin to foam. Add remaining 1/2 cup (125 mL) sugar and beat, on high speed, until stiff peaks form; fold in coconut.

Spread over cake batter, smoothing meringue to touch the edges of the pan. Bake on the middle rack at 325°F (160°C) for 50 minutes.

Gooseberry Fool Cake

Gooseberries are large, tart, green berries that once grew wild in many areas of the country. Gooseberries were often eaten in luscious fools, which married the unique taste of the berries with rich whipped cream.

FOOL

3 cups (750 mL)	ripe gooseberries
1/4 cup (50 mL)	elderflowers (optional)
1/4 cup (50 mL)	Muscat wine
1/4 cup (50 mL)	granulated sugar
1 cup (250 mL)	whipping cream

ASSEMBLY

1 recipe	genoise
	(see page 11)
1/2 recipe	rich custard
	(see page 9), cooled
1/2 recipe	buttercream
	(see page 3)

For fool: Remove the blossom ends from the gooseberries and discard.

In a heavy-bottomed pan over low heat, heat berries and elderflowers for 5 minutes. Puree and pass through a sieve. Stir wine and 2 tbsp (25 mL) sugar into berries and refrigerate for 2 hours.

In a stainless steel bowl, whip cream with remaining sugar and set aside.

To assemble: Cut genoise into two 8-inch (20 cm) rounds. Cover 1 layer with custard and place second layer on top. Use buttercream to ice the sides of the cake, and smooth gooseberry fool over the top of the cake.

Serve immediately.

Grandmother Foster's Lemon Pound Cake

Mary Lou Harrison is a fellow member of The Women's Culinary Network and, to help in my quest to discover Canada's best cake recipes, Mary Lou provided her grandmother's recipe for lemon pound cake. She remembers, "No visit from my Grandmother Foster was complete without the presentation of a lemon pound cake. My brother and I both vied for the middle and end pieces, which were always especially lemony. Grandma enjoyed slices of this cake as part of a 'night lunch' after a good game of Scrabble or cards with friends."

CAKE

1/3 cup (75 mL)	butter, softened
1 cup (250 mL)	granulated sugar
2	eggs, room temperature
1/2 cup (125 mL)	2% milk, room temperature
1 1/2 cups (375 mL)	all-purpose flour
1 1/2 tsp (7 mL)	baking powder
1/4 tsp (1 mL)	salt
	zest of 1 lemon, grated

GLAZE

1/3 cup (75 mL)	icing sugar
6 tbsp (90 mL)	lemon juice

For cake: Cream butter and sugar. Stir in eggs and milk.

In a small bowl, combine flour, baking powder, salt and lemon zest.

Stir dry ingredients into creamed mixture until just combined.

Pour into a greased and floured loaf pan and bake on the middle rack at 350°F (180°C) for 40 to 45 minutes or until a tester comes out clean.

For glaze: In a bowl, combine icing sugar with lemon juice and pour over hot cake. Remove carefully from pan when cake has cooled.

Our Professional Best

If there is one thing I love about the industry I work in, it's the people. The food is pretty phenomenal, it's true, and I am also fond of the many excuses to drink champagne—but really it's the people. From the fresh young pastry chefs, with their energy and bright ideas, to the seasoned chefs with their impressive knowledge and bearing to the food writers with their amazing spirit and generosity, they're a lovely bunch.

And they can bake! The recipes in this chapter reflect the work of many of Canada's best food professionals. These people are well trained and passionate about their work—and it shows. Here you will find recipes for meringue tortes, blueberry buckle, amaretti cheesecake and, of course, a few cakes featuring the most wonderful of flavors, chocolate.

Chocolate Meringue Torte with Grand Marnier Cream

I cannot write a book without including a recipe from my own favorite lady of words and culinary deeds, Rose Murray. This recipe first appeared in Rose Murray's Comfortable Kitchen Cookbook, in which she wrote, "This easy make-ahead dessert has such a delightful flavor and texture that it's bound to be a real hit at any dinner party."

MERINGUES

8	egg whites
1/4 tsp (1 mL)	cream of tartar
pinch	salt
1 tsp (5 mL)	pure vanilla extract
1 1/2 cups (375 mL)	fruit sugar or granulated sugar processed in a blender until fine

ASSEMBLY

1 cup (250 mL)	semisweet chocolate chips
2 cups (500 mL)	whipping cream
1/4 cup (50 mL)	Grand Marnier or other orange liqueur chocolate curls, for garnish

For meringues: Cover 2 baking sheets with parchment or brown paper. On paper, draw three 9-inch (23 cm) circles.

In a large bowl, beat egg whites until frothy. Beat in cream of tartar, salt and vanilla until soft peaks form. Very gradually beat in sugar until stiff peaks form.

Spoon mixture onto circles, smoothing tops with spatula.

Bake at 250°F (120°C) for 1 hour; turn off oven and let meringues cool in oven for at least 6 hours or overnight.

Using a metal spatula, carefully remove meringues from paper.

To assemble: Melt chocolate chips and spread over 2 meringue layers.

In a bowl, whip cream; beat in liqueur.

Place 1 chocolate-covered meringue on serving plate and spread with one-third of the cream. Top with a plain meringue, then half of the remaining cream. Place second chocolate-covered meringue on top; spread with remaining cream.

Garnish with chocolate curls. Cover loosely and chill for 24 hours before serving. (If there's any moisture on the plate at serving time, blot with paper towel.)

Apricot Platz with Maple Cream

Jane Langdon of the Wine Country Cooking School in Niagara-on-the-Lake suggests substituting an equal amount of sliced rhubarb for the apricot. Obtain information about her unique cooking school/winery online at www.winecountrycooking.com.

CAKE

1 1/2 cups (375 mL)	all-purpose flour
2 tsp (10 mL)	baking powder
1/2 cup (125 mL)	granulated sugar
1/2 cup (125 mL)	cold butter, cubed
1/2 cup (125 mL)	milk

TOPPING

3 cups (750 mL)	sliced, pitted apricots
1/3 cup (75 mL)	maple syrup
1/4 cup (50 mL)	brown sugar
1/2 cup (125 mL)	all-purpose flour
2 tbsp (25 mL)	butter

MAPLE CREAM

2 to 3 tbsp (25 to 50 mL)	maple syrup
1/2 cup (125 mL)	low-fat sour cream

For cake: In medium bowl, mix together flour, baking powder and sugar. Cut 1/2 cup (125 mL) butter into flour mixture with pastry blender. Stir in milk.

Pat batter into a greased 8-inch (2 L) square pan.

For topping: Combine apricots with 1/3 cup (75 mL) maple syrup. Spoon over batter.

Mix brown sugar and flour in a small bowl and cut in butter until mixture is crumbly. Sprinkle crumb topping over fruit.

Bake at 350°F (180°C) for 40 to 50 minutes, until golden brown.

For maple cream: Whisk maple syrup and sour cream together. Refrigerate, covered, until ready to serve.

Serve cake warm or at room temperature. Cut into squares and top with a spoonful of maple cream.

Blueberry Buckle

Food writer and stylist Heather Trim comments, "Enjoyed for breakfast or dessert, this cake is quick to prepare and works well with frozen blueberries too. If you do use frozen berries, don't thaw them."

TOPPING

1/2 cup (125 mL)	brown sugar
1/2 cup (125 mL)	all-purpose flour
1/2 tsp (2 mL)	cinnamon
1/3 cup (75 mL)	cold butter, cubed

CAKE

1 1/2 cups (375 mL)	all-purpose flour
1 tsp (5 mL)	baking powder
1/4 tsp (1 mL)	baking soda
1/4 tsp (1 mL)	freshly ground nutmeg
1/4 tsp (1 mL)	salt
3/4 cup (175 mL)	butter, room temperature
	zest of 1 lemon, finely grated
3/4 cup (175 mL)	granulated sugar
2	eggs
1/2 cup (125 mL)	sour cream or plain yogurt
1 tsp (5 mL)	pure vanilla extract
2 cups (500 mL)	blueberries

For topping: In a small bowl, stir brown sugar, flour and cinnamon. Using your fingertips, rub in butter until coarse crumbs form; set aside.

For cake: Whisk together flour, baking powder, baking soda, nutmeg and salt until combined; set aside.

In the bowl of an electric mixer, beat butter with lemon zest and sugar on high speed until light. Reduce speed to medium and beat in eggs, one at a time, until combined.

Beat in sour cream and vanilla. Reduce speed to low and beat in flour mixture just until combined. Fold in blueberries.

Scrape batter into a buttered 9-inch (2.5 L) square pan and smooth surface. Sprinkle with topping.

Bake at 375°F (180°C) until cake starts to pull away from sides of pan and a tester comes out clean, about 35 to 40 minutes. Serve hot, warm or cold.

Pineapple Carrot Cake

Baker Dawn Hallman of Patterson-Kaye Lodge in Bracebridge, Ontario, says of this all-in-one cake, "I love recipes like this dessert, which are basically one step, quick and easy."

1 1/2 cups (375 mL)	all-purpose flour
1 cup (250 mL)	granulated sugar
3/4 cup (175 mL)	crushed pineapple, with juice
2	medium carrots, grated
1/2 cup (125 mL)	vegetable oil
2	eggs
1 tsp (5 mL)	baking powder
1 tsp (5 mL)	baking soda
1 tsp (5 mL)	pure vanilla extract
1 recipe	cream cheese icing (see page 8)

Place flour, sugar, pineapple, carrots, oil, eggs, baking powder, baking soda and vanilla in a medium bowl and stir until just moistened.

Turn into 2 buttered and floured 8-inch (1.2 L) cake pans. Bake on the middle rack at 350°F (180°C) for 35 minutes or until a tester comes out clean.

Cool for 10 minutes, then remove from pan.

When completely cool, frost with cream cheese icing.

Deep Chocolate Cake

Dawn Hallman of Patterson-Kaye Lodge, Muskoka, recommends looking for the best-quality cocoa you can find for this moist one-step cake—the better the cocoa, the better the cake.

1 3/4 cups (425 mL)	all-purpose flour
2 cups (500 mL)	granulated sugar
3/4 cup (175 mL)	cocoa
1 cup (250 mL)	milk
2	eggs
1/2 cup (125 mL)	vegetable oil
1 1/2 tsp (7 mL)	baking soda
1 1/2 tsp (7 mL)	baking powder
1/4 tsp (1 mL)	salt
1 cup (250 mL)	boiling water
1 recipe	chocolate buttercream (see page 5) or whipped chocolate ganache (see page 18)

Place flour, sugar, cocoa, milk, eggs, oil, baking soda, baking powder and salt in a medium bowl and mix until smooth. Stir in boiling water. Mixture will be very thin.

Turn into 2 greased and floured 8-inch (1.2 L) cake pans.

Bake on the middle rack at 350°F (180°C) for 35 minutes or until a tester comes out clean.

Cool for 10 minutes, then remove from pans.

Let cool completely, then fill and frost with chocolate buttercream or whipped ganache.

Raspberry Pear Coffee Cake

Judson Simpson is executive chef at the House of Commons and the manager of Culinary Team Canada. Canada's regional and national culinary teams have been in the top five internationally since 1984. We already knew Canadian cuisine was world class— now we've got the medals to prove it.

TOPPING

1/4 cup (50 mL)	Grape-Nuts cereal
3 tbsp (50 mL)	granulated sugar
2 tbsp (25 mL)	chopped pecans
1/2 tsp (2 mL)	cinnamon

CAKE

2 cups (500 mL)	all-purpose white flour
3/4 cup (175 mL)	granulated sugar
4 tsp (20 mL)	baking powder
1 tsp (5 mL)	cinnamon
1/2 tsp (2 mL)	salt
1	large egg
1 cup (250 mL)	buttermilk
3 tbsp (50 mL)	canola oil or vegetable oil
1 tsp (5 mL)	pure vanilla extract
2	medium Bartlett pears, cut in wedges, skin left on
1/2 cup (125 mL)	fresh or frozen and thawed unsweetened raspberries

In a small bowl, stir together Grape-Nuts, sugar, pecans and cinnamon; set aside.

In a medium bowl, stir together the flour, sugar, baking powder, cinnamon and salt.

In a large bowl, whisk together the egg, buttermilk, oil and vanilla. Add the flour mixture to the egg mixture and stir the batter just to blend.

Pour batter into a 9-inch (2.5 L) springform pan that has been coated with nonstick spray.

Arrange pear wedges over the batter and place raspberries in the center. Sprinkle the Grape-Nuts mixture evenly over top of the fruit.

Bake on the middle rack at 400°F (200°C) for 40 to 45 minutes, or until the top is golden brown and a tester comes out clean.

Let cool for 10 minutes, loosen edges and remove from pan.

Serve hot, warm or cold.

Mairlyn's World-Famous Chocolate Fudge Cake

Mairlyn Smith's cooking is familiar to many through her cookbook Lick the Spoon and her television show Food for Thought. She and I are birds of a feather, and when we think cake, we think chocolate.

CAKE

1 2/3 cups (400 mL)	all-purpose flour
1 1/2 cups (375 mL)	granulated sugar
2/3 cup (150 mL)	dutched cocoa
1 1/2 tsp (7 mL)	baking soda
1/2 cup (125 mL)	shortening, cubed, room temperature
1 cup (250 mL)	water
1/2 cup (125 mL)	milk
2 tsp (10 mL)	lemon juice
2	large eggs
1 tbsp (15 mL)	pure vanilla extract

FUDGE ICING

8 oz (240 g)	semisweet chocolate (the better the quality, the better the bowl-licking after!)
1/2 cup (125 mL)	dutched cocoa
3/4 cup (175 mL)	water
1/2 cup (125 mL)	unsalted butter
3 cups (750 mL)	icing sugar

For cake: In a large mixing bowl, stir together the flour, sugar, cocoa and baking soda. Add shortening.

In a medium bowl, mix together the water, milk, lemon juice, eggs and vanilla. Pour into the flour mixture and, using an electric mixer, mix on low till combined, approximately 30 seconds. Scrape the bowl down.

Turn the mixer to medium and mix for 2 1/2 minutes. Scrape the bowl once. Do not overmix.

Divide the batter equally between 3 greased, parchment-lined 8-inch (1.2 L) pans and spread evenly.

Bake at 350°F (180°C) for 35 to 40 minutes or until a tester comes out clean.

Cool in the pan for 10 minutes. Run a knife around the edge of the pan, then flip cakes onto a cooling rack and let cool completely.

For icing: In a saucepan, combine the chocolate, cocoa, water and butter and stir until melted. Remove from heat.

Add the icing sugar and stir till combined. Pour the mixture into a bowl and put it in the fridge until thick, about 3 to 4 hours.

When thick, beat for 1 to 3 minutes or until creamy then fill and frost layers with icing.

Lick spoon and bowl while standing over the sink. Be sure to wash your face before leaving the house.

The cake can be made up to this point 2 days before serving time as long as it is covered. Also freezes well for up to 1 month.

Blueberry Almond Cake

Debbie Diament runs a hands-on cooking school in her Toronto home. To learn more, visit her website at www.myplacefordinner.com. She writes about this recipe, "Blueberries cover an almond-flavored cake with a cookie-like texture. Great for dessert, for tea, or to pack on a picnic."

1/2 cup (125 mL)	unsalted butter, softened
2/3 cup (150 mL)	granulated sugar
1	egg
1 tsp (5 mL)	pure vanilla extract
1/2 tsp (2 mL)	almond extract
1 1/4 cups (300 mL)	all-purpose flour
1/2 tsp (2 mL)	baking powder
1/4 tsp (1 mL)	salt
2 cups (500 mL)	fresh or frozen blueberries
1 tbsp (15 mL)	sugar
1/4 tsp (1 mL)	cinnamon

In a large bowl, cream butter and 2/3 cup (150 mL) sugar until well blended. Add egg, vanilla and almond extract and beat until pale and creamy.

In a separate bowl, combine flour, baking powder and salt. Add to batter and beat until well mixed. Don't overwork the batter.

Chill 30 minutes, or until the batter is no longer wet and sticky.

Press batter into the bottom and sides of a buttered 9-inch (2.5 L) springform or 10-inch (25 cm) buttered tart pan with a removable rim.

Mix blueberries with 1 tbsp (15 mL) sugar and cinnamon and sprinkle over batter.

Bake on the middle rack at 350°F (180°C) for 40 minutes, or until cake is golden brown.

Cool 5 minutes on a wire rack, then place the tart pan on an inverted bowl and pull down the rim. Return the pan to the rack and cool completely, about 1 1/2 hours, before serving.

Apple Cake with Balsamic Glaze

Dana McCauley's apple cake is a unique twist on a Canadian favorite.
The balsamic glaze is perfectly suited to the cake and completely original.

CAKE

1/2 cup (125 mL)	granulated sugar
1 tsp (5 mL)	cinnamon
4	Granny Smith apples, peeled and thinly sliced
4	egg yolks, beaten
2/3 cup (150 mL)	sour cream
1 tsp (5 mL)	pure vanilla extract
2 cups (500 mL)	cake and pastry flour
1 cup (250 mL)	granulated sugar
1/2 tsp (2 mL)	baking soda
1/2 tsp (2 mL)	baking powder
1/2 tsp (2 mL)	freshly ground nutmeg
pinch	salt
3/4 cup (175 mL)	butter, softened

GLAZE

3/4 cup (175 mL)	apple juice
1/4 cup (50 mL)	balsamic vinegar

For cake: Toss sugar, cinnamon and apples together. Spread out in well buttered 9-inch (2.5 L) springform pan; reserve.

In a separate bowl, stir together yolks, 1 tbsp (15 mL) of the sour cream and vanilla; reserve.

Stir together flour, sugar, baking soda, baking powder, nutmeg and salt in a large bowl.

Add butter and remaining sour cream and blend, using an electric mixer set to low speed, until dry ingredients begin to clump. Increase speed to high and beat for 1 1/2 minutes.

Add egg mixture, beating well and scraping down sides of bowl.

Drop spoonfuls of batter into prepared pan; gently smooth surface.

Bake at 350°F (180°C) for 40 to 45 minutes or until a tester comes out clean.

Cool cake in pan on a wire rack for 10 minutes; turn onto a serving plate.

For glaze: Boil apple juice and balsamic vinegar in saucepan set over medium heat for about 12 minutes or until reduced to a syrup. Brush evenly over cake.

Serve warm or cold.

Mocha Angel Cake with Mascarpone Filling

Dana McCauley's angel cake wins on two counts: It is both stunning to look at and delightful to taste. Coffee, sinful smooth mascarpone cheese and fresh raspberries are a taste combination that is difficult to match.

CAKE

3/4 cup (175 mL)	cake and pastry flour
1 1/2 cups (375 mL)	granulated sugar
1/4 cup (50 mL)	cocoa
16	egg whites
1 tsp (5 mL)	instant coffee granules
1 tbsp (30 mL)	lemon juice
1 tsp (5 mL)	cream of tartar
1 tsp (5 mL)	pure vanilla extract
1/2 tsp (2 mL)	salt

FILLING

1 1/2 cups (375 mL)	whipping cream
3 tbsp (50 mL)	marmalade or apricot jam
2 tsp (10 mL)	finely chopped crystallized ginger
1 cup (250 g)	mascarpone cheese
2 cups (500 mL)	raspberries or other soft fruit
	mint leaves, orange peel twists or chocolate curls, for garnish

For cake: In a large bowl, stir flour with 3/4 cup (175 mL) sugar and cocoa; reserve.

In a clean glass or stainless steel bowl, beat egg whites until foamy. Dissolve coffee in lemon juice, then add with cream of tartar, vanilla and salt to egg whites. Beat until soft peaks form. Still beating, gradually add remaining 3/4 cup (175 mL) of sugar until glossy, stiff peaks form.

Gently fold flour mixture, one-quarter at a time, into egg whites until well blended.

Spoon batter into an ungreased 10-inch (4 L) tube pan with removable bottom, and run a spatula through the batter to eliminate any large air pockets. Smooth top.

Bake on the middle rack at 350°F (180°C) for about 40 minutes or until cake springs back when lightly touched.

Turn pan upside down and balance edges on two cans or legs attached to pan until completely cool.

For filling: Meanwhile, beat whipping cream, marmalade and ginger until soft peaks form. Add mascarpone and beat until very thick.

To assemble: Run a knife around the edge of the pan and remove cake. Using a serrated knife, cut cake into 2 layers. Place bottom layer on a platter.

Spread with one-third of mascarpone mixture and top with half the berries. Spread another third of the mascarpone mixture on the bottom of next layer and place cake on top of fruit. Spread remaining mascarpone mixture evenly over top of cake and arrange remaining berries on top.

Garnish with mint leaves and orange peel twists or chocolate curls.

Gâteau Opéra

Joanne Leese trained as a pastry chef at San Francisco's renowned Tante Marie Cooking School. She has baked in some of Toronto's most critically acclaimed restaurants and is now a freelance food consultant. She writes, "To me, Gâteau Opéra is pure decadence!"

CAKE

1 1/2 cups (375 mL)	almonds
1/3 cup (75 mL)	all-purpose flour
3	egg yolks
1/2 tsp (2 mL)	pure vanilla extract
2/3 cup (150 mL)	granulated sugar
4	egg whites
1/4 cup (50 mL)	melted butter

COFFEE BUTTERCREAM

4	egg yolks
1/2 cup (125 mL)	granulated sugar
1/3 cup (75 mL)	water
1 cup (250 mL)	butter
4 tsp (20 mL)	dried instant coffee

GANACHE MOUSSE

1/2 cup (125 mL)	milk
8 oz (240 g)	semisweet or bittersweet chocolate, chopped into pieces
1 cup (250 mL)	whipping cream

GLAZE

1/2 cup (125 mL)	whipping cream
2 tsp (10 mL)	corn syrup
6 oz (180 g)	chocolate, chopped into pieces

SIMPLE SYRUP

1/4 cup (50 mL)	granulated sugar
1/4 cup (50 mL)	boiling water
1 tbsp (15 mL)	strong coffee
	melted chocolate, for garnish

For cake: Using a food processor, process nuts and flour until powdery; reserve.

Beat egg yolks with vanilla and 1/3 cup (75 mL) of sugar until thick and light.

In a clean glass or stainless steel bowl, whip egg whites until stiff, then add the remaining 1/3 cup (75 mL) sugar, beating until stiff and glossy.

Quickly and lightly fold the flour/nut mixture alternately with the egg whites into the egg yolk mixture in 2 to 3 batches. Add the butter when most of the final flour is mixed in and mix.

Spread batter evenly into a buttered and floured, parchment-lined 15- x 10-inch (2 L) jelly roll pan and bake at 350°F (180°C) for 8 to 10 minutes. Remove from the oven, and let cool in the pan before cutting it.

For coffee buttercream: Beat egg yolks lightly until mixed. Heat sugar with water until dissolved. Boil until syrup reaches the soft ball stage (239°F/115°C on a sugar thermometer).

Gradually pour the hot sugar syrup onto egg yolks, beating constantly, and continue beating until the mixture is cool and thick.

In a separate bowl, cream butter and then gradually beat it into egg mixture until smooth and creamy. Dissolve coffee in 2 tsp (10 mL) hot water and allow to cool. Beat in coffee. Use within 1 hour.

For ganache mousse: Bring milk to a boil. Remove from heat, and stir in chocolate until it is completely melted. Cool until just warm but still liquid.

Whip cream to soft peaks and lightly fold into chocolate mixture until thoroughly mixed. Refrigerate until ready to use.

For glaze: Bring cream and corn syrup to a boil over a high heat. Remove from heat and stir in the chocolate until it is melted completely. Use within 1 hour.

For simple syrup: Dissolve sugar in boiling water. Remove from heat and add coffee.

To assemble: Using a serrated knife, slice the cake horizontally into thirds, and brush each piece with the simple syrup. Place one layer of the almond cake on a cardboard cake base. Top this layer with a 1/8-inch (0.25 cm) thickness of buttercream.

Top that layer with another layer of almond cake. Spread a 1/4-inch (0.5 cm) thickness of ganache mousse on the top. Top the mousse with the last almond cake. Spread a thin layer of buttercream on top of this layer, just to barely cover. Refrigerate the cake until firm.

Warm the glaze slightly until it is as thick as honey. Glaze the top of the cake, and refrigerate again until the glaze is set.

Using a long sharp knife, trim the edges of the cake evenly so that the sides are exposed. With a little melted chocolate, pipe "Opéra" on the top of the cake and underline it.

Refrigerate for several hours or overnight before serving. Trim the cardboard cake base down so that it is flush with the edge of the cake and does not show. This cake is best eaten after it has chilled for at least 24 hours, and up to 2 days. Let it come to room temperature before slicing.

Welsh Tea Loaf

Home economist Joan Ttooulias says this loaf is perfect for teatime. It keeps best wrapped in parchment and foil, stored in a cool, dry place.

3 cups (750 mL)	mixed dried currants, raisins and sultanas
1 cup (250 mL)	granulated sugar
1 1/4 cups (300 mL)	warm, brewed tea
1	egg, room temperature
2 rounded tbsp (40 mL)	thick-cut marmalade
2 cups (500 mL)	all-purpose flour
2 cups (500 mL)	whole wheat flour
4 tsp (20 mL)	baking powder

In a large bowl, soak the dried fruit and sugar in warm tea overnight.

Mix in egg and marmalade. Combine flours with baking powder and stir into fruit mixture. Spoon batter into 2 greased and parchment-lined 8- x 4-inch (1.5 L) loaf pans and smooth batter.

Bake at 325°F (160°C) for 1 1/2 hours or until a tester comes out clean.

Cool in pans on rack. Allow to mature for a few days before serving, thinly sliced and buttered.

Belgian Cake

Home economist Joan Ttooulias invented this technique, where dough is grated onto the top of the cake for a very pretty effect. The dough must be chilled to a firm consistency and grated on the course side of the grater. She also suggests using fruit sugar rather than granulated since it is finer and dissolves well in cake batters and meringues.

1 cup (250 mL)	unsalted butter, softened
1/4 cup (50 mL)	granulated sugar
1	egg
2 tbsp (25 mL)	vegetable oil
1 tsp (5 mL)	pure vanilla extract
4 cups (1 L)	all-purpose flour
1 tsp (5 mL)	baking powder
1/4 tsp (1 mL)	salt
2/3 cup (150 mL)	raspberry, strawberry, apricot or plum jam
	icing sugar, for garnish

Cream butter and sugar until light and fluffy. Beat in egg, oil and vanilla.

Combine flour, baking powder and salt and fold in. Knead gently to form a dough and chill dough, if necessary, for 30 minutes or until it is firm enough to grate.

Divide dough in half; grate half into a greased and floured 8-inch (1.2 L) pan. Spoon jam over. Grate remaining dough over jam.

Bake on the middle rack at 350°F (180°C) for 60 to 70 minutes or until lightly browned.

Immediately dust generously with icing sugar and cool on a rack.

Serve warm or cold.

Amaretti Cheesecake

Home economist Joan Ttooulias is the source of this spectacular cheesecake, which combines cream cheese with wonderfully rich mascarpone. Fans of this Italian triple cream cheese can also try Deb's Walnut Mascarpone Coffee Cake on page 66.

CRUST

1/3 cup (75 mL)	unsalted butter, melted
16	digestive biscuits, crushed
1/3 cup (75 mL)	unblanched almonds, finely chopped

FILLING

1 cup (500 mL)	cream cheese, softened
1/2 cup (125 mL)	mascarpone cheese
1/4 cup (50 mL)	granulated sugar
2	eggs, separated
1 tsp (5 mL)	pure vanilla extract
1 tbsp (15 mL)	cornstarch
1/2 cup (125 mL)	sour cream
12	amaretti biscuits, coarsely crushed
4 cups (1 L)	strawberries, for garnish
1/3 cup (75 mL)	granulated sugar

For crust: In a bowl, mix together butter, crushed digestive biscuits and almonds. Press mixture into bottom and partially up sides of a greased 8-inch (2 L) springform pan. Set aside.

For filling: Beat together cream cheese, mascarpone and sugar until smooth. Beat in egg yolks, vanilla, cornstarch and sour cream.

Whisk egg whites until they hold soft peaks. Stir one-third of the egg whites into cheese mixture and then carefully fold in the remaining egg whites.

Pour mixture into pan and scatter amaretti crumbs on top.

Bake at 300°F (150°C) for 1 1/2 hours or until firm to touch.

Turn off heat and allow cheesecake to cool in oven for 2 hours before removing springform sides.

Serve with sliced strawberries tossed in sugar.

Raspberry Chocolate Roulade

Home economist Joan Ttooulias suggests that this roulade can be used at Christmas as a Buche de Noel; simply decorate with fresh holly leaves and meringue mushrooms.

ROULADE

6	eggs, separated
3/4 cup (175 mL)	granulated sugar
3/4 cup (175 mL)	cocoa, sifted

FILLING

1/2 cup (125 mL)	whipping cream, whipped
1 cup (250 mL)	rich custard (see recipe on page 9)
2 cups (500 mL) (approx.)	fresh raspberries

ASSEMBLY

1 1/2 cups (375 mL)	whipping cream
2 tbsp (25 mL)	granulated sugar
1 tsp (5 mL)	pure vanilla extract
	cocoa
	fresh raspberries, for garnish
	chocolate leaves, for garnish

For roulade: Whisk egg yolks until thickened and pale yellow. Beat in sugar until dissolved. Fold in cocoa.

In a clean glass or stainless steel bowl, whisk egg whites until they hold soft peaks. Spoon one-third of the egg whites into egg yolk mixture and then fold in remaining egg whites. Spoon into a greased 13- x 9-inch (3.5 L) parchment-lined pan.

Bake at 350°F (180°C) for 20 minutes or until risen and puffy. When the cake comes out of the oven, it will sink slightly. Cool completely on rack. Turn cake out onto a sheet of parchment slightly larger than the roulade, which has been dusted with icing sugar.

For filling: Stir 1/2 cup (125 mL) whipped cream and custard together. Spread cream mixture onto roulade. Top with raspberries. Roll up roulade lengthwise into a long roll and cover with parchment paper. Refrigerate for at least 2 hours.

Remove parchment paper from roulade, and carefully place roulade onto a serving dish.

To assemble: Beat 1 1/2 cups (375 mL) whipping cream with sugar and vanilla until just firm enough to either pipe or spread over roulade. Dust with cocoa and decorate with fresh raspberries and chocolate leaves.

Chocolate Hazelnut Torte

Kim Groomes is pastry chef at Delta Grandview's Resort in Huntsville, Ontario. Kim is a brilliant young pastry chef making her mark in the industry, and her desserts have customers clamoring for more.

CAKE		ASSEMBLY	
1/2 cup (125 mL)	butter	1 cup (250 mL)	35% cream, whipped
1 cup (250 mL)	granulated sugar	1 tsp (5 mL)	icing sugar
6 oz (180 g)	semisweet chocolate	1 tsp (5 mL)	granulated sugar
5	eggs, separated	1 tsp (5 mL)	Frangelico
1 cup (250 mL)	ground hazelnuts		(hazelnut-flavored
1/4 tsp (1 mL)	salt		liqueur)
		4 cups (1 L)	strawberries, quartered
		1/3 cup (75 mL)	granulated sugar
			icing sugar, for garnish

For cake: Melt butter, sugar and chocolate in a bowl over simmering water. Stir until smooth.

Remove from heat and add the egg yolks and hazelnuts. Stir in well with a wooden spoon.

In a clean glass or stainless steel bowl, beat the egg whites and salt until stiff peaks form. Fold the whites into the chocolate mixture one-third at a time.

Pour into a greased 9-inch (2.5 L) springform pan and bake on the middle rack at 350°F (180°C) for 35 minutes or until a tester comes out clean.

Cool and turn out onto a rack.

To assemble: Combine the whipped cream, 1 tsp (5 mL) icing sugar, granulated sugar and Frangelico.

Toss berries with sugar. Sift icing sugar over the cake and serve with the berries and cream mixture.

Mrs. Reid's Plain Cake

Food editor Lucy Waverman published this recipe in the Cooking School Cookbook.
She writes, "Originally from a Mrs. Reid from the Arnprior area, this cake is a staple in
my family. It is a moist, buttery, plain cake, which could find a home in everyone's
repertoire. Serve it with strawberries and ice cream or cut into layers and
frosted with a chocolate or plain icing."

1/2 cup (125 mL)	butter, room temperature
1 cup (250 mL)	granulated sugar
2	eggs
1 tsp (5 mL)	pure vanilla extract
1 1/2 cups (375 mL)	all-purpose flour
1 1/2 tsp (7 mL)	baking powder
1/2 tsp (2 mL)	salt
1/2 cup (125 mL)	milk

In a large bowl, with an electric mixer or by hand, cream together the butter and sugar until light and fluffy. Beat in eggs, one at a time, and vanilla; reserve.

In a separate bowl, sift together the flour, baking powder and salt.

Mix dry ingredients and milk into egg mixture alternately, one-third of the flour mixture and half of the milk at a time, beginning and ending with dry ingredients.

Spoon batter into a greased 9-inch (2.5 L) square pan. Bake on the middle rack at 375°F (190°C) for 35 minutes, or until a tester comes out clean.

Maple Pear Upside-down Cake

Emily Richards, co-host of Canadian Living Cooks, writes of her recipe, "This stunning cake brings the sweetness of maple syrup to pears. This would work just as well with baking apples. Use a dark amber pure maple syrup for best results. Serve with whipped cream."

TOPPING			
1/3 cup (75 mL)	maple syrup	2	eggs
1/4 cup (50 mL)	packed brown sugar	1 tbsp (15 mL)	pure vanilla extract
1/4 cup (50 mL)	chopped toasted pecans	1 1/2 cups (375 mL)	all-purpose flour
3	ripe Bosc or Bartlett pears	1 tsp (5 mL)	cardamom or cinnamon
		1 tsp (5 mL)	baking powder
CAKE		1/2 tsp (2 mL)	baking soda
1/2 cup (125 mL)	butter, softened	pinch	salt
3/4 cup (175 mL)	packed brown sugar	1/2 cup (125 mL)	sour cream

For topping: In small saucepan, heat maple syrup and brown sugar over medium-high heat until mixture begins to bubble. Boil gently for 1 minute, stirring. Pour into greased 9-inch (2.5 L) pan. Sprinkle with pecans.

Peel, quarter, core and cut pears lengthwise into 1/4-inch (0.5 cm) slices. Arrange pears over maple mixture in concentric circles overlapping each other slightly; set aside.

For cake: In large bowl, beat butter and brown sugar until fluffy. Add eggs one at a time, beating after each addition. Beat in vanilla.

In another bowl, combine flour, cardamom, baking powder, baking soda and salt.

Mix dry ingredients and sour cream into egg mixture alternately, one-third of the flour mixture and half of the sour cream at a time, beginning and ending with dry ingredients.

Scrape batter into pan over pears. Smooth batter carefully without moving pears. Bake at 350°F (180°C) for about 45 minutes or until a tester comes out clean. Let cool in pan on rack for 20 minutes. Invert cake pan onto serving plate and remove cake pan. Scrape any maple glaze from pan onto cake.

Schnitz or Farmer's Fruitcake

Edna Staebler is a national treasure whose talent with language and people led her to write cookbooks celebrating Canadian Mennonite cuisine. She wrote about dried apple schnitz, "Every autumn Eva spends days peeling, coring and schnitzing apples: she spreads the apple segments on pans in the oven and on top of her big black wood-stove; and when they are thoroughly dry and crisp she stores them in sacks in an upstairs room where they'll keep for months, becoming spongy and chewy." The schnitz is then eaten as a snack or baked into pie and cake. Here is Edna's recipe, written in her own wonderful style.

2 cups (500 mL)	dried apple schnitz		4 cups (1 L)	flour
2 cups (500 mL)	molasses		1 tsp (5 mL)	cinnamon
1 cup (250 mL)	butter or lard		1 tsp (5 mL)	allspice
2 cups (500 mL)	brown sugar		1/2 tsp (2 mL)	freshly ground nutmeg
2	eggs, well beaten		2 tsp (10 mL)	baking soda
1 cup (250 mL)	buttermilk or sour milk			

Soak the apples overnight in water. In the morning, drain them and put them through a food chopper (or processor).

Simmer the apples in the molasses with the butter for 1 hour. "If you don't put the butter in, the apples will form into a hard taffy ball," Eva told me.

When the apples have cooled, add the brown sugar, well-beaten eggs, buttermilk, flour, cinnamon, allspice, nutmeg and baking soda.

Pour into a 13- x 9-inch (3.5 L) pan and bake at 350°F (180°C) for 1 hour or until a tester comes out clean.

The top will be crusty and chewy and doesn't need icing, which might detract from the fantastic flavor.

Pam's Zucchini Chocolate Cake

Ottawa's Pam Collacott originally published this recipe in her book, PamCooks. Look for other recipes on her website at www.pamcooks.com. She writes, "This is a lovely, moist chocolate cake, perfect for packed lunches. I always demonstrate it in cooking classes at the end of the summer, when everyone has a garden full of zucchinis the size of canoes."

1/4 cup (50 mL)	butter or margarine, softened
3/4 cup (175 mL)	granulated sugar
3 tbsp (45 mL)	oil
1	egg
1/2 tsp (2 mL)	pure vanilla extract
3 tbsp (50 mL)	sour milk or buttermilk
2 1/2 tbsp (37 mL)	cocoa
1/4 tsp (1 mL)	baking powder
1/2 tsp (2 mL)	baking soda
1/4 tsp (1 mL)	cinnamon
1 1/4 cups (300 mL)	all-purpose flour
1 cup (250 mL)	finely grated zucchini
1/4 cup (50 mL)	chocolate chips

Cream together the butter and sugar until smooth. Stir in the oil, egg, vanilla and sour milk and beat well.

In a separate bowl, stir the cocoa, baking powder, baking soda, cinnamon and flour together, then add it to the butter mixture. Stir in the zucchini and mix well.

Pour the batter into a lightly greased 8-inch (1.2 L) pan. Smooth the top and sprinkle the chocolate chips over top.

Bake on the middle rack at 350°F (180°C) for about 25 minutes, or until a tester comes out clean.

Note: When a recipe calls for sour milk, use 1 tsp (5 mL) of lemon juice or vinegar to sour 1 cup (250 mL) milk. Sour milk can be replaced with buttermilk or buttermilk powder dissolved in water. (Buttermilk powder can be purchased in bulk food stores and should be kept in an airtight container in a cool place.)

Special Occasion Cakes

Cake is so much more than flour, butter, egg, sugar and spices;
cake represents ritual and celebration. We bake cakes to honor our rites
of passage—our birthdays, graduations and weddings. We bake a cake as
a display of affection, a way to pamper guests and elevate the
everyday to something a little more wonderful.

This chapter highlights a few of the many cakes we bake to make special
occasions more special. Christmas fruitcakes were one of my earliest favorites,
so I've included two versions of that holiday treat here, as well as my own
Christmas cake, which is part of my perfect feast.

And there are weddings. The wedding cake is a subject vast enough to
fill many, many books, and indeed it does. When presented with the task
for a family wedding, I opted for a French croquembouche, but pastry chef
Joanne Leese's favorite wedding cake, complete with buttercream
and fondant, is the highlight of this chapter.

Caramel Meringue Christmas Cake

This cake is an adaptation of Rose Murray's recipe from page 108. I further simplified this elegant cake and then gilded it with caramel. All white and gold, it's a lovely cake for Christmas.

MERINGUES			ASSEMBLY	
8	egg whites		2 cups (500 mL)	whipping cream
1/4 tsp (1 mL)	cream of tartar		1/3 cup (75 mL)	granulated sugar
pinch	salt		1 tsp (5 mL)	pure vanilla extract
1 tsp (5 mL)	pure vanilla extract			
1 1/2 cups (375 mL)	fruit sugar or granulated sugar processed in a blender until fine			
1 recipe	caramel (see page 16)			

For meringues: Cover 2 baking sheets with parchment or brown paper. On paper, draw three 9-inch (23 cm) circles.

In a clean glass or stainless steel bowl, beat egg whites until frothy. Beat in cream of tartar, salt and vanilla until soft peaks form. Very gradually, beat in sugar until stiff peaks form. Spoon mixture onto circles, smoothing tops with spatula.

Bake at 250°F (120°C) for 1 hour; turn off oven and let meringues cool in oven for at least 6 hours or overnight.

Using a metal spatula, carefully remove meringues from paper.

Using caramel, drizzle thin lines over meringues. Pour the rest of the caramel over a parchment-covered flat surface and let cool; break into shards and set aside until needed.

To assemble: Whip cream; beat in sugar and vanilla. Place 1 caramel-covered meringue on serving plate, and spread with one-third of the cream. Top with second meringue, then half of the remaining cream. Place third caramel-covered meringue on top, and spread with remaining cream. Garnish with caramel shards.

Steamed Cranberry Pudding

Chris Fenton of Windsor, Ontario, writes this about her grandmother's cranberry pudding: "My grandma, Dorothy Hines, made this cake every Christmas for as long as I can remember, and my mom has been making it since Grandma passed away. I never really liked it much as a kid, but I remember the adults going on and on about it, and them saying how I'd like it when I got older. They were right. I love it and cannot imagine Christmas without it. My grandma (and mom) usually use cleaned-out tin cans as the molds for these puddings. And then the 'logs' are cut into slices, so the pieces are circles. However, any 'quart mold' and slicing technique would do."

PUDDING

2 tsp (10 mL)	baking soda
1/2 cup (125 mL)	molasses
1/2 cup (125 mL)	boiling water
1 1/2 cups (375 mL)	sifted all-purpose flour
1 tsp (5 mL)	baking powder
1 cup (250 mL)	fresh cranberries
1 tbsp (15 mL)	flour

GORGEOUS SAUCE

1/2 cup (125 mL)	granulated sugar
1/2 cup (125 mL)	whipping cream (or half-and-half)
1/4 cup (50 mL)	butter

For pudding: In a large bowl, add baking soda to molasses then stir in boiling water.

In a separate bowl, sift flour, then add baking powder and sift again. Add molasses mixture.

Toss cranberries in flour and mix into batter.

Pour batter into a greased 1 quart (1 L) mold. Cover and steam for 30 minutes in a pressure cooker.

Without pressure cooker: Pour 2 inches (5 cm) boiling water into a pan large enough to hold mold with space around it. Place a rack in the bottom of a pan and position the mold on the rack.

Place on the middle rack and bake at 350°F (180°C) for 2 hours. Replenish boiling water as needed.

For sauce: Combine sugar, cream and butter in a medium saucepan and heat over medium heat for 15 minutes or until thick. Do not boil.

To assemble: To reheat sauce, warm over medium heat, stirring constantly so that it doesn't separate, and pour over pudding.

Victorian Christmas Cake

Cordon Bleu-trained Sandra Cranston-Corradini teaches everything from outdoor entertaining to advanced French cuisine at her cooking school near Alliston, Ontario. She writes, "The 1800s recipes for fruitcake surpass any modern recipes. I substitute maple syrup for some of the sugar for a distinctly Canadian touch."

6 cups (1.5 L)	light raisins		2 tsp (10 mL)	baking powder
4 cups (1 L)	glazed cherries		4 cups (1 L)	blanched, halved almonds
2	green pineapple rings, diced		1 cup (250 mL)	sweetened, shredded coconut
6 cups (1.5 L)	candied mixed peel		1 1/2 cups (375 mL)	brandy
2 cups (500 mL)	candied orange peel		1/2 tsp (2 mL)	salt
4 cups (1 L)	all-purpose flour		2 tsp (10 mL)	rose water or
2 cups (500 mL)	butter		2 tsp (10 mL)	grated lemon zest
4 1/2 cups (1.1 L)	granulated sugar		6 drops	oil of lemon
10	eggs			

Toss raisins, cherries, pineapple, mixed peel and orange peel with the flour and set aside overnight.

In a medium bowl, cream butter and sugar; add the eggs and continue to mix well.

In a large bowl, mix the baking powder, almonds, coconut, brandy, salt, rose water, oil of lemon and dried fruit and add to the egg mixture.

Scrape batter into 2 parchment-lined, 8-inch (1.2 L) pans and bake on the middle rack at 350°F (180°C) for 1 to 1 1/2 hours, or until a tester comes out clean.

Cool in pans.

Victorian Dark Christmas Cake

Sandra Cranston-Corradini is a woman of many culinary talents, one of which is writing for In the Hills *magazine. She has also been a series host and chef/writer for* A Day in the Country Television *on Life Network. This is a nineteenth-century recipe from her family archives.*

6 cups (1.5 L)	currants	1 tsp (5 mL)	freshly ground nutmeg
6 cups (1.5 L)	raisins	1 tsp (5 mL)	cloves
9	pineapple rings, diced	2 cups (500 mL)	butter
2 cups (500 mL)	halved glazed cherries	2 cups (500 mL)	granulated sugar
2 cups (500 mL)	shredded citron peel	12	well-beaten eggs
2 cups (500 mL)	sherry or grape juice	3 cups (750 mL)	blanched almonds
4 1/2 cups (1.1 L)	all-purpose flour	4 1/2 cups (1.1 L)	pecans, broken
1 tbsp (15 mL)	cinnamon	1 tbsp (15 mL)	pure vanilla extract
2 tsp (10 mL)	allspice	3/4 cup (175 mL)	grape jelly

Pick over the currants, raisins, pineapple rings, cherries and peel to remove stems and leaves. Place in a large bowl and mix thoroughly. Soak overnight in sherry or juice.

In a separate bowl, sift flour, cinnamon, allspice, nutmeg and cloves together 3 times.

In another bowl, beat butter, then add sugar, creaming until light and fluffy. Add the fruit mixture and mix thoroughly.

Mix dry ingredients and eggs into the fruit mixture alternately, one-third of the flour mixture and half of the eggs at a time, beginning and ending with dry ingredients.

Add the almonds and pecans gradually, distributing them throughout the batter.

Add vanilla and grape jelly.

Bake in four 9-inch (1.5 L) pans on the middle rack at 325°F (160°C) for 1 to 1 1/2 hours, or until a tester comes out clean.

Allow to cool in the pans.

Favorite Wedding Cake

The most elaborate cake most people experience, and the one they will always remember, is usually a wedding cake. Pastry chef Joanne Leese has made more than her share of brilliant cakes, but this one is tops in her book. Joanne writes, "This is the first wedding cake I ever made and it remains a favorite. The fondant gives it a really smooth finish, the pale yellow polka dots add some fun and the pearl trim gives it a sophisticated finish. I have included a recipe for the rolled fondant, but it can be easily purchased in any specialty cake supply store." The cake yields 25 small slices.

CAKE

4 cups (1 L)	sifted cake and pastry flour
4 tsp (20 mL)	baking powder
1/4 tsp (1 mL)	salt
1 cup (250 mL)	butter, room temperature
1 3/4 cups (425 mL)	granulated sugar
6	egg yolks, room temperature
2 tsp (10 mL)	pure vanilla extract
1 1/2 cups (375 mL)	milk

APRICOT FILLING

1/2 cup (125 mL)	dried apricots
1 cup (250 mL)	hot water
1/2 cup (125 mL)	granulated sugar

BUTTERCREAM

4	egg whites
1 1/4 cups (300 mL)	granulated sugar
1 1/2 (375 mL) to 2 cups (500 mL)	butter, cubed and softened

ROYAL ICING

1 1/2 cups (375 mL)	icing sugar
1	egg white
1/2 tsp (2 mL)	lemon juice

ROLLED FONDANT

half envelope	unflavored gelatin
1/4 cup (50 mL)	cold water
1/2 cup (125 mL)	glucose
1 tbsp (15 mL)	glycerin
2 tbsp (25 mL)	solid vegetable shortening
8 cups (2 L) (approx.)	icing sugar
2 to 3 drops	yellow food coloring
	crystallized flowers

For cake: Sift the flour with the baking powder and salt, and set aside.

Cream the butter and sugar until light and fluffy. Beat in the egg yolks, mixing until thoroughly incorporated. Add the vanilla.

Mix dry ingredients and milk into egg mixture alternately, one-third of the flour mixture and half the milk at a time, beginning and ending with dry ingredients. Stir until smooth.

Pour the batter into one 6-inch (750 mL) and one 9-inch (1.5 L) pan, which have been lined with parchment, greased and floured.

Bake at 375°F (190°C) for 40 to 45 minutes.

Cool the cakes in the pans for 10 minutes, and then remove from pans and cool completely, approximately 2 hours, on a wire rack. Set aside.

For apricot filling: In a small heavy saucepan, cover apricots with hot water; let stand for 1 hour or until softened. Add sugar. Bring apricots, sugar and water to boil; cover and simmer until tender, 10 to 15 minutes. Drain, transfer to food processor or blender and puree apricots. Set aside.

For buttercream: In a large bowl, combine egg whites and sugar. Stir gently with a whisk over a hot water bath until the mixture is hot to the touch. Remove from heat and continue beating until cool and stiff. Whisk butter into the cooled meringue one cube at a time, fully incorporating each piece before next addition. Set aside.

For royal icing: Using an electric mixer, beat icing sugar, egg white and lemon juice together until stiff peaks form. If not using immediately, cover with a damp cloth to prevent a crust from forming.

For fondant: Combine gelatin and cold water, and let stand until spongy. Place the bowl of gelatin over a hot water bath and heat until dissolved. Add the glucose and glycerin and mix well. Stir in the shortening and stir until almost completely melted. Remove from heat and cool the mixture to lukewarm.

In the bowl of an electric mixer, pour 4 cups (1 L) of the icing sugar and make a well in the center. Pour the lukewarm gelatin mixture into the well and beat gently with paddle attachment until thoroughly mixed.

Add icing sugar, a little at a time, until the stickiness disappears. Turn the mixture out of the mixing bowl, and knead in enough of the remaining sugar to form a smooth, soft, pliable dough that does not stick to your hands. If fondant is too soft, add more sugar; if too stiff, add water one drop at a time.

Use the fondant immediately or store in airtight container (not refrigerated) indefinitely.

To assemble: Using a serrated knife, trim tops of cake layers to make them even. Cut each cake in half horizontally, as evenly as possible.

Spread a 1/4-inch (0.5 cm) layer of buttercream over each bottom layer of cake. Next, spread half the apricot filling over each bottom layer. Place top layers on top.

Using a palette knife, cover each cake's sides and tops with a very thin layer of buttercream.

Sprinkle a rolling surface with plenty of icing sugar and roll out two pieces of fondant, one for each cake, about 1/8- to 1/4-inch (0.25 to 0.5 cm) thick. Roll each piece of fondant onto your rolling pin, and unroll it over the cake.

Cut the excess off in a wide circle around the base of each cake. Gently press the fondant around the sides of the cake, ensuring that it is smooth. Trim the fondant flush with the base of the cake.

Using a few dabs of royal icing, secure the 9-inch (23 cm) cake on a cake board and leave it to dry for several hours or overnight (unrefrigerated).

Using a pastry bag filled with royal icing, pipe small pearls, shells or stars around the bottom edges of the cake.

Cut 5 plastic straws or wooden dowels to the exact height of bottom cake. These dowels will act as supports for the top cake. Insert one straw at the center of the bottom cake and insert remaining straws, centered and evenly spaced, to support the 6-inch (15 cm) cake.

Center the 6-inch (15 cm) cake on the bottom cake and use royal icing to attach the smaller cake in the center of the 9-inch (23 cm) cake.

Using the remaining royal icing, pipe small pearls, shells or stars around the bottom edges of the smaller cake.

Knead a piece of fondant with 2 or 3 drops or food coloring to make pale yellow.

Roll out the colored fondant and cut out 1-, 2- and 3-inch (2.5, 5 and 7.5 cm) circles. Place the small circles all over the cake to make a polka-dot design. Let the wedding cake dry overnight, and finish with some tiny crystallized flowers.

Halloween Pumpkin Cheesecake

Ghouls and goblins will delight in this seasonal dessert that serves up a little nutrition along with the requisite holiday sweetness.

CRUST

1/4 cup (50 mL)	butter, melted
1 1/2 cups (375 mL)	gingersnap cookie crumbs

FILLING

1 cup (250 mL)	cream cheese, room temperature
3/4 cup (175 mL)	brown sugar
1 cup (250 mL)	canned or cooked and mashed pumpkin

3	eggs
1 tsp (5 mL)	pure vanilla extract
2 tbsp (25 mL)	white chocolate liqueur
1 tsp (5 mL)	ginger
1 tsp (5 mL)	cinnamon
1/4 tsp (1 mL)	allspice
1/4 tsp (1 mL)	salt

ASSEMBLY

1 cup (250 mL)	whipping cream
1 tbsp (15 mL)	granulated sugar

For crust: In a medium bowl, combine butter and cookie crumbs; press into the bottom of a buttered 9-inch (2.5 L) springform pan. Bake in the lower third of the oven at 350°F (180°C) for 5 minutes. Remove from oven.

For filling: In a large bowl, beat cream cheese and brown sugar together until smooth. Beat in pumpkin, then eggs, one at a time. Stir in vanilla, liqueur, ginger, cinnamon, allspice and salt.

Pour into prepared pan and bake on the middle rack at 350°F (180°C) for 20 minutes or until set around the edges. Turn off heat and allow to cool in oven for 50 minutes. Refrigerate.

To assemble: Whip cream with sugar and pipe or spoon along edge of cake.

Honeyed Almond Coffee Cake

I happily celebrate everyday experiences and love to make breakfast a special occasion. Honeyed almonds can be found in most bulk stores. Search out a good-quality bulk store in your area, where stock is fresh and regularly rotated.

FILLING

1 3/4 cups (425 mL)	honeyed almond pieces
1/3 cup (75 mL)	packed brown sugar
2 tbsp (25 mL)	grated orange zest
1/2 tsp (2 mL)	freshly ground nutmeg

CAKE

3 cups (750 mL)	all-purpose flour
2 tsp (10 mL)	baking powder
1 tsp (5 mL)	baking soda
1/4 tsp (1 mL)	salt
1/2 tsp (2 mL)	freshly ground nutmeg
3/4 cup (175 mL)	unsalted butter, softened
1 cup (250 mL)	packed brown sugar
3/4 cup (175 mL)	granulated sugar
3	eggs, room temperature
3 tbsp (50 mL)	orange liqueur
2 tsp (10 mL)	pure vanilla extract
1 1/2 cups (375 mL)	sour cream

For filling: In a small bowl, combine honeyed almond pieces, brown sugar, zest and nutmeg; set aside.

For cake: In a large bowl, stir together flour, baking powder, baking soda, salt and nutmeg, then sift.

Cream butter until light; add brown sugar and granulated sugar and continue creaming until the mixture is light and fluffy. Beat in eggs, one at a time, then liqueur and vanilla.

Mix dry ingredients and sour cream into egg mixture alternately, one-third of the flour mixture and half of the sour cream at a time, beginning and ending with dry ingredients.

Turn into a greased and floured 10-inch (4 L) tube pan, alternating batter with filling mixture, and ending with batter.

Bake on the middle rack at 350°F (180°C) for 1 hour or until a tester comes out clean.

The Great Canadian Cake Contest

We have our winner! Readers at Canadian Online Explorer (CANOE) wrote in with their best cake recipes, and we did the hard work of tasting their delicious submissions. Choosing one winner was tough—there were so many great cakes to select from.

However, our overall winner was Spiced Devil's Food Cake, sent in by Sandra Post of Prince George, British Columbia; it's a wonderful combination of moist chocolate cake, aromatic spices and rich mocha icing. Sandra's recipe is accompanied by two honorable mentions: a sumptuous, creamy cheesecake and a sponge cake with a whipped cream filling. Delicious!

Thanks to everyone who sent in recipes—we loved trying them.

Spiced Devil's Food Cake

This recipe was submitted by Sandra Post of Prince George, British Columbia.

CAKE

1 cup (250 mL)	butter, softened
2 cups (500 mL)	granulated sugar
4	eggs
1 tsp (5 mL)	pure vanilla extract
2 cups (500 mL)	all-purpose flour
1/4 cup (50 mL)	cocoa
1 tsp (5 mL)	baking powder
1 tsp (5 mL)	baking soda
1 tsp (5 mL)	cinnamon
1/2 tsp (2 mL)	freshly grated nutmeg
1/2 tsp (2 mL)	cloves
1 cup (250 mL)	buttermilk

ICING

3 3/4 cups (925 mL)	icing sugar
1/4 cup (50 mL)	cocoa
6 tbsp (90 mL)	strong coffee
6 tbsp (90 mL)	butter, melted
1 tsp (5 mL)	pure vanilla extract
	whole almonds, optional

For cake: In a mixing bowl, cream butter and sugar. Add eggs, one at a time, beating well after each egg. Add vanilla.

Sift together flour, cocoa, baking powder, baking soda, cinnamon, nutmeg and cloves.

Mix dry ingredients and buttermilk into egg mixture alternately, one-third of the flour mixture and half of the buttermilk at a time, beginning and ending with dry ingredients.

Pour into 2 greased and floured 9-inch (1.5 L) cake pans.

Bake on the middle rack at 350°F (180°C) for 30 to 35 minutes or until a tester comes out clean.

For icing: Mix icing sugar, cocoa, strong coffee, melted butter and vanilla until smooth. Add another tablespoon of coffee if necessary to obtain a smooth, spreadable texture.

To assemble: Frost 1 cake layer, top with second layer and frost sides and top of cake. Garnish with almonds, if desired.

Butter Tart Cheesecake

This recipe was submitted by J. Gail Phillips of Kingston, Ontario.

CRUST
1 cup (250 mL)	all-purpose flour
1 tbsp (15 mL)	granulated sugar
1 tbsp (15 mL)	packed brown sugar
pinch	salt
1/2 cup (500 mL)	cold butter, cubed

FILLING
3 cups (750 g)	cream cheese, room temperature
1/2 cup (125 mL)	granulated sugar
1/2 cup (125 mL)	brown sugar
1 tsp (5 mL)	pure vanilla extract

3	eggs
1 cup (250 mL)	sour cream
2 tbsp (25 mL)	all-purpose flour
1/4 tsp (1 mL)	salt

SAUCE
1 1/2 cups (375 mL)	brown sugar
1/2 cup (125 mL)	butter
3 tbsp (50 mL)	half-and-half cream or milk
1	egg, beaten
1 tsp (5 mL)	pure vanilla extract
pinch	salt

For crust: Combine flour, granulated sugar, brown sugar and salt; cut in butter. Knead until dough begins to come together, then press into a greased and floured 10-inch (3 L) springform pan.

Bake on the middle rack at 325°F (160°C) for 20 minutes. Remove from oven and allow to cool.

For filling: Beat together cream cheese, granulated sugar, brown sugar and vanilla until well blended. Beat in eggs and sour cream. Stir in flour and salt until blended.

Pour onto cooled crust and bake on the middle rack at 350°F (180°C) for 35 to 40 minutes or until edges begin to darken but center is still jiggly. Allow to cool in the oven with the door propped open. Refrigerate for 3 hours or overnight.

For sauce: Mix brown sugar, butter, cream, egg, vanilla and salt in a heavy-bottomed pot. Cook over medium-high heat until mixture begins to boil. Reduce heat to medium and cook, stirring, for 1 minute. Remove from heat and allow to cool.

To assemble: Pour cooled sauce over cake and serve immediately.

Chocolate Cream Cake

This recipe was submitted by Veronica Beer of London, Ontario.

CAKE

2	eggs, separated
1 cup (250 mL)	granulated sugar
1 tsp (5 mL)	pure vanilla extract
2 tbsp (30 mL)	warm water
1/2 cup (125 mL)	flour
1/2 cup (125 mL)	cornstarch
1 tsp (5 mL)	baking powder

FILLING

3 cups (750 mL)	whipping cream
1 cup (250 mL)	icing sugar
1 package (9 g)	vanilla sugar
2 tbsp (25 mL)	cocoa

ICING

1 cup (250 mL)	icing sugar
2 tbsp (25 mL)	cocoa
2 tbsp (25 mL) (approx.)	hot water
1 tbsp (15 mL)	melted butter
1 tbsp (15 mL)	shaved chocolate, for garnish

For cake: Whisk egg yolks with 1/4 cup of sugar, vanilla and warm water until thick and creamy.

Using a clean glass or stainless steel bowl, whisk egg whites with remaining 3/4 cup (175 mL) sugar until stiff peaks. Fold whites into yolk mixture.

Whisk together flour, cornstarch and baking powder and sift into yolk mixture, gently folding in.

Turn into a greased and floured 10-inch (3 L) springform pan and bake in the lower third of the oven at 350°F (180°C) for 12 to 15 minutes or until golden. Remove from oven and cool in pan.

For filling: Whip cream until stiff. Set aside 3 tbsp (50 mL) whipped cream for decoration.

Whisk together icing sugar, vanilla sugar and cocoa then fold into the whipped cream until combined.

For icing: Sift together icing sugar and cocoa, then add water and melted butter to achieve a stiff but spreadable consistency.

To assemble: Turn the cooled cake upside down, then cut horizontally into 2 layers. Spread filling over layers, and then stack them. Coat the sides of the cake with icing.

Pipe the reserved whipped cream onto the top of the cake in a star shape and press shaved chocolate onto the sides of the cake.

Low-Fat Cakes

In "The Science behind Cake," I discussed the vital role that fat plays in the moist butter cake of our dreams. Although these high-fat, scrumptious cakes are an important part of our rituals and celebrations, there are times when a lower fat recipe is required. These cakes are for those days when you really are sticking to your health food choices; when comfort doesn't require whipped cream on top and when you feel light as a cloud and simply don't want to be weighed down.

This chapter visits the fat-free angel food cake, healthy snacking cakes, a twist on creamy cheesecake (sans cream) and some cakes made with heart-smart canola oil.

Angel Food Cake

This is the grandmama of all low-fat cakes. Because angel food cakes rely on air whipped into egg white for leavening, they contain no fat at all and yet they are delightfully light and tender. The cake can be served very simply with no more than fresh fruit, or sliced into layers with whipped cream and buttercream filling. I love a combination of the two: simple cake with fresh fruit and gobs of whipped cream.

1 cup (250 mL)	cake and pastry flour
1 1/2 cups (375 mL)	granulated sugar
1/4 tsp (1 mL)	salt
12	extra-large egg whites
1 tsp (5 mL)	cream of tartar
1 tsp (5 mL)	pure vanilla extract

Sift together flour, 3/4 cup (175 mL) sugar and salt, 3 times.

In a large, clean glass or stainless steel bowl, beat egg whites with cream of tartar on low speed until they begin to foam. Increase speed to medium and slowly add remaining 3/4 cup (175 mL) sugar, beating until whites are stiff and have increased in volume five times. Beat in vanilla.

Sift one-quarter of the flour mixture into the egg whites and gently fold in with a rubber spatula. Repeat 3 times.

Turn into an ungreased 10-inch (4 L) angel food pan (ideally with a removable bottom) and gently run a spoon once through the batter to release any air bubbles.

Bake immediately on the middle rack at 350°F (180°C) for 35 minutes or until cake springs back to the touch.

Let cool, inverted, perched on a bottle, 4 glasses or on the feet of an angel food pan, for 2 hours or until completely cool. Gravity will keep the cake from collapsing.

Keep pan inverted as you loosen the cake from the sides of the pan and the tube with a knife. Release pan or coax cake out with a few taps.

Orange Ginger Cheesecake

This cake is full of fresh flavors and refreshing spice, rather than a lot of fat. Its name comes from its cheesecake-like texture. In fact, there isn't any cheese in it at all.

2 cups (500 mL)	plain, nonfat yogurt
1 cup (250 mL)	orange juice
2 tsp (10 mL)	minced orange zest
1 tsp (5 mL)	minced lemon zest
2	large eggs, separated
1/2 cup (125 mL)	granulated sugar
1/2 cup (125 mL)	all-purpose flour
1/2 tsp (2 mL)	ginger
pinch	cloves
1/2 cup (125 mL)	nonfat sour cream
1/2 tsp (2 mL)	pure vanilla extract
1	large, seedless orange

Place yogurt in a cheesecloth-lined strainer and drain over a bowl overnight in the refrigerator.

In a saucepan, cook orange juice and zests over medium-high until reduced to 1/4 cup (50 mL), about 10 minutes; chill.

In a mixing bowl, beat egg yolks and sugar together. Combine flour, ginger and cloves and stir into yolk mixture.

In another bowl, combine yogurt, juice mixture, sour cream and vanilla, then stir into yolk mixture.

In a clean glass or stainless steel bowl, beat egg whites until stiff, then fold into yolk mixture.

Turn into a parchment-lined 9-inch (2.5 L) springform pan and bake on the middle rack at 350°F (180°C) for 30 minutes or until set.

Refrigerate cooled cake for several hours or overnight. Loosen cake sides from pan with a knife before removing sides.

Slice orange into thin, horizontal slices and arrange in concentric circles on top of cake.

Lower Fat Banana Raisin Loaf

This recipe reflects my own approach to low-fat eating: because I simply cannot forego delicious foods like butter, I eat smaller portions less often. So, although there is butter and egg yolk in this cake, it's only one-quarter of the butter I would normally use. Works for me!

1/4 cup (50 mL)	butter
1/2 cup (125 mL)	granulated sugar
3	eggs
1 cup (250 mL)	ripe bananas, mashed (2 to 3 bananas)
1/4 cup (50 mL)	apricot puree (found in the baby food section of the supermarket)
1 tsp (5 mL)	pure vanilla extract
1/4 cup (50 mL)	molasses
1 3/4 cups (425 mL)	all-purpose flour
2 tsp (10 mL)	baking powder
1/2 tsp (2 mL)	baking soda
1/4 tsp (1 mL)	salt
1/2 cup (125 mL)	raisins
1 tbsp (15 mL)	all-purpose flour

In a large bowl, cream together butter and sugar until pale and fluffy. Beat in eggs, one at a time, until smooth. Add banana, apricot puree, vanilla and molasses; mix.

In another bowl, sift together flour, baking powder, baking soda and salt; fold into liquid mixture in thirds. Toss raisins in flour and fold into batter.

Turn into a greased and floured 8- x 4-inch (1.5 L) loaf pan and bake on the middle rack at 350°F (180°C) for 1 hour and 15 minutes or until a tester comes out clean.

Cool on a rack.

Nanny's Low-Fat Muffins

The only reason I am able to write at all with two small children is thanks to the help of my children's part-time nanny, Joan Lyddiatt. Joan's high cholesterol count has led her to devise satisfying, low-fat recipes like this one. My son loves these muffins for their taste and texture, and never suspects that he's eating something that is actually healthy.

2	medium ripe bananas, mashed
1 cup (250 mL)	buttermilk
4	egg whites, lightly beaten
2 cups (500 mL)	whole wheat flour
1 1/2 cups (375 mL)	raisin bran cereal
1 tsp (5 mL)	baking soda
1 tsp (5 mL)	baking powder
1 tsp (5 mL)	cinnamon

In a large bowl, thoroughly mix bananas, buttermilk and egg whites.

In a separate bowl, combine flour, raisin bran cereal, baking soda, baking powder and cinnamon.

Stir together dry and wet ingredients and spoon into a nonstick muffin tin.

Bake on the middle rack at 350°F (180°C) for 20 to 25 minutes or until a tester comes out clean.

Cool on a rack.

Light and Luscious Carrot Lemon Cloud Cake

Gaye Musselman of Woodland Springs B&B Penlake in Muskoka writes, "This cake, with no fat and only half a cup of flour, is a popular choice with guests. If you want a lighter accompaniment, serve instead with fat-free frozen yogurt."
Visit Gaye at ***www.penlake-woodlandsprings.com.***

CAKE

1 1/4 cups (300 mL)	granulated sugar
1 tsp (5 mL)	salt
5 to 6	medium carrots, peeled
	juice and zest of
	large lemon
5	egg yolks, beaten till
	fluffy
1/2 cup (125 mL)	flour
1 cup (250 mL)	ground almonds
2 tsp (10 mL)	pure vanilla extract
6	egg whites

TOPPING

1 cup (250 mL)	whipping cream
1/2 cup (125 mL)	granulated sugar
1/4 tsp (1 mL)	almond flavoring
1 cup (250 mL)	sliced almonds, toasted

For cake: In a large saucepan, dissolve 1/4 cup (50 mL) of sugar and 1 tsp (5 mL) of salt in 5 cups (1.25 L) of water. Add carrots and boil in sugared water for 15 to 20 minutes or until soft. Drain carrots, pat dry, then grate in a food processor. You should have 1 cup (250 mL) packed down. Allow carrots to cool.

Transfer carrots to a large bowl and mix in remaining 1 cup (250 mL) of sugar, lemon juice and zest. Add egg yolks, flour, almonds and vanilla and mix until combined.

In a clean glass or stainless steel bowl, beat egg whites until stiff but not dry. Fold batter into egg whites.

Gently turn into a 9-inch (2.5 L) springform pan that has been coated with nonstick spray and bake on the middle rack at 350°F (180°C) for 1 hour or until spongy to the touch.

Refrigerate and serve cold.

For topping: Before serving, whip cream with sugar and almond flavoring. Fill and frost cake with cream mixture and garnish with toasted almonds.

Maple Cake with Maple Glaze

This cake, from the Canola Council of Canada's ABCs of Cooking with Canola, is not only low in overall fat content (4 g per serving) but also very low in saturated fat.

1 tbsp (15 mL)	canola oil
3 tbsp (50 mL)	granulated sugar

CAKE

3/4 cup (175 mL)	applesauce
2 cups (500 mL)	all-purpose unbleached flour
1 1/2 tsp (7 mL)	baking powder
1 1/2 tsp (7 mL)	baking soda
1/2 tsp (2 mL)	salt
2 tsp (10 mL)	cinnamon
1	large egg, lightly beaten

2/3 cup (150 mL)	brown sugar
1/3 cup (75 mL)	pure maple syrup
1/3 cup (75 mL)	cider vinegar
1/3 cup (75 mL)	vanilla yogurt
3 tbsp (50 mL)	canola oil

GLAZE

1 1/2 cups (375 mL)	icing sugar, sifted
1 tsp (5 mL)	pure vanilla extract
1/4 cup (50 mL) (approx.)	pure maple syrup

Use the canola oil to coat the inside of a 10-inch (2.5 L) bundt pan. Sprinkle with 3 tbsp (50 mL) granulated sugar and shake out excess.

For cake: Pour applesauce into a sieve set over a measuring cup and drain for a few minutes. You should have 1/2 cup (125 mL).

In large mixing bowl, blend together flour, baking powder, baking soda, salt and cinnamon; set aside.

In another bowl, whisk together applesauce, egg, brown sugar, maple syrup, vinegar, yogurt and 3 tbsp (50 mL) canola oil. Add dry ingredients to the liquid mixture, and stir until flour is just moistened. Turn into prepared pan.

Bake at 375°F (190°C) for 10 to 12 minutes or until top of cake springs back when touched lightly. Loosen edges and remove; turn cake onto a rack to cool.

For glaze: In a small bowl, combine icing sugar and vanilla. Gradually whisk in enough maple syrup to make a glaze of coating consistency. Drizzle glaze over cake to coat. Allow to set before serving.

Sunday-Best Chocolate Cake

It's chocolate and it's low-fat! This chocolate cake, with only 5.1 grams of fat per serving, was developed for Canola Cooks! A Culinary Celebration of Canola. *For more canola recipes see the Canola Information Service website at* www.canolainfo.org.

1 1/2 cups (375 mL)	granulated sugar
2/3 cup (150 mL)	canola oil
2	eggs
2 tsp (10 mL)	pure vanilla extract
2 2/3 cups (650 mL)	all-purpose flour
2/3 cup (150 mL)	cocoa
2 tsp (10 mL)	baking powder
2 tsp (10 mL)	baking soda
1 tsp (5 mL)	salt
2 cups (500 mL)	boiling water

In a large bowl, beat sugar, canola oil, eggs and vanilla for 4 minutes.

In a separate bowl, sift together flour, cocoa, baking powder, baking soda and salt.

Mix dry ingredients and boiling water into egg mixture alternately, one-third of the flour mixture and half of the boiling water at a time, beginning and ending with dry ingredients.

Pour into an oiled and floured 13- x 9-inch (3.5 L) cake pan.

Bake on the middle rack at 350°F (180°C) for 40 minutes or until cake springs back to the touch.

Tiramisu

Carry me up (which is what tira mi su means in Italian) to a world of divine decadence where rich, creamy desserts are served with plenty of nice boozy biscuits and good, strong coffee. Tiramisu is traditionally made with rich mascarpone cheese, which is a triple-cream buttery delight that weighs in at about 45% fat content. My recipe from Nice Timing: Gourmet Meals in Minutes substitutes ricotta at 2% to 5% fat, and the dessert is still delicious. However, if you don't mind the calories and you think tiramisu made without mascarpone is a sin, feel free to slather it on the liqueur-soaked biscuits and enjoy.

4	large ladyfingers
	(see recipe on page 13)
1/4 cup (50 mL)	strong brewed coffee or espresso
2 tbsp (25 mL) + 2 tsp (10 mL)	coffee liqueur
1/3 cup (75 mL)	whipping cream
2/3 cup (150 mL)	ricotta cheese
1 tbsp (15 mL)	granulated sugar
pinch	cinnamon
pinch	freshly ground nutmeg
2 tbsp (25 mL)	grated chocolate, for garnish

Trim 2 large ladyfingers to fit the bottom of a 5 3/4 x 3 1/4 (625 mL) mini loaf pan.

Soak the cookies with 2 tbsp (25 mL) coffee and 2 tbsp (25 mL) coffee liqueur. The biscuits should absorb all the liquid.

In a large bowl, whip the cream until it is stiff. In a separate bowl, cream the ricotta and sugar together until the mixture is smooth. Add cinnamon and nutmeg; stir in whipped cream.

Spoon half of this mixture over soaked cookies and place the remaining ladyfingers on top. Pour the remaining coffee and liqueur over cookies. Spoon the remaining cheese mixture over the top and cover with grated chocolate.

Place in the refrigerator to set for 2 hours.

Beet and Carrot Cake

*Home economist Simone Demers Collins from the Canola Information Service offered
the following four recipes, in which the saturated fat has been replaced with canola oil,
and added vegetables provide a nutritional boost.*

2 cups (500 mL)	all-purpose flour, sifted
1 tbsp (15 mL)	baking powder
1/4 tsp (1 mL)	salt
1 tsp (5 mL)	cinnamon
3	eggs, separated
3/4 cup (175 mL)	canola oil
1 1/2 cups (375 mL)	granulated sugar
1 tsp (5 mL)	pure vanilla extract
3 tbsp (50 mL)	hot water
1 cup (250 mL)	raw carrots, finely grated
1 cup (250 mL)	beets, raw or cooked, grated
1/2 cup (125 mL)	walnuts, chopped, optional
	icing sugar, for garnish

In a medium bowl, sift flour, baking powder, salt and cinnamon. Set aside.

In a clean glass or stainless steel bowl, beat egg whites until stiff; reserve.

In a large bowl, using an electric mixer, blend canola oil and sugar. Add egg yolks, vanilla and
hot water. Beat well.

Beat flour mixture into oil mixture. Add carrots, beets and walnuts. Fold in egg whites. Spread
batter into a lightly oiled 13- x 9-inch (3.5 L) baking pan and bake at 350°F (180°C) for 45 to 55
minutes or until a tester comes out clean. Cool on wire rack.

When ready to serve, dust with a sprinkle of icing sugar.

Sauerkraut Chocolate Cake

Home economist Simone Demers Collins was part of the team that created this lighter version of a most unusual recipe. Simone told me that many of the people who have tried this cake think the sauerkraut is actually long strands of coconut. Perhaps we should retitle it Chocolate Surprise Cake.

2 1/4 cups (550 mL)	all-purpose flour, sifted
1/2 cup (125 mL)	dutched cocoa
1 tsp (5 mL)	baking powder
1 tsp (5 mL)	baking soda
1/4 tsp (1 mL)	salt
3/4 cup (175 mL)	canola oil
1 1/2 cups (375 mL)	granulated sugar
3	large eggs
1 tsp (5 mL)	pure vanilla extract
1 cup (250 mL)	strong coffee or water
3/4 cup (175 mL)	sauerkraut, rinsed, drained, and coarsely chopped
1 recipe	mocha buttercream (see page 6)

In a medium bowl, combine the flour, cocoa, baking powder, baking soda and salt; set aside.

In a large bowl, blend canola oil and sugar. Add eggs, one at a time, beating well after each addition. Add vanilla.

Mix dry ingredients and coffee or water into egg mixture alternately, one-third of the flour mixture and half the coffee or water at a time, beginning and ending with dry ingredients. Beat well after each addition. Beat in the sauerkraut.

Divide batter between 2 lightly oiled and floured 8-inch (1.2 L) pans.

Bake at 350°F (180F) for 25 to 30 minutes or until a tester comes out clean.

Allow cakes to cool, then fill and frost with mocha buttercream.

Zucchini Chocolate Cake

Simone Demers Collins enjoys this cake as is, but also suggests achieving a finer texture in the cake by substituting cooked and pureed zucchini.

CAKE

2 cups (500 mL)	all-purpose flour
1/4 cup (50 mL)	dutched cocoa
1 tsp (5 mL)	baking powder
1 tsp (5 mL)	baking soda
1 tsp (5 mL)	cinnamon
1/2 tsp (2 mL)	freshly ground nutmeg
1/2 tsp (2 mL)	salt
3	large eggs
2 cups (500 mL)	granulated sugar
1/2 cup (125 mL)	canola oil
1 tsp (5 mL)	grated orange zest
1 tsp (5 mL)	pure vanilla extract
3/4 cup (175 mL)	buttermilk
2 cups (500 mL)	raw zucchini, shredded
1 cup (250 mL)	walnuts or pecans, chopped

GLAZE

1 cup (250 mL)	icing sugar
5 tsp (25 mL)	orange juice
1 tsp (5 mL)	shredded orange zest
1 tbsp (15 mL)	margarine, melted

For cake: In a medium bowl, sift together flour, cocoa, baking powder, baking soda, cinnamon, nutmeg and salt. Set aside.

In large bowl, beat eggs until very light. Gradually beat in sugar until mixture is fluffy. Slowly beat in canola oil, orange zest and vanilla.

Mix dry ingredients and buttermilk into egg mixture alternately, one-third of the flour mixture and half the buttermilk at a time, beginning and ending with dry ingredients. Stir in zucchini and walnuts.

Turn into 2 oiled 9-inch (1.5 L) pans and bake on the middle rack at 350°F (180°C) for 40 to 45 minutes or until a tester comes out clean.

Set cake on racks to cool for 10 minutes.

For glaze: In medium bowl, stir icing sugar, orange juice, shredded orange zest and melted margarine until smooth and drizzle over warm cake.

Rutabaga Cake

People don't expect rutabaga in their cake, yet this recipe was a hit with local chefs at Alberta's Restaurant and Food Exhibition. Rutabagas are the winter cousins of summer's white turnips.

CAKE

2 1/2 cups (625 mL)	all-purpose flour
1 tsp (5 mL)	baking soda
1 tsp (5 mL)	baking powder
2 tsp (10 mL)	cinnamon
1/2 tsp (2 mL)	salt
3	eggs
1/2 cup (125 mL)	canola oil
1/4 cup (50 mL)	buttermilk
3/4 cup (175 mL)	granulated sugar
2 tsp (10 mL)	pure vanilla extract

1 can (14 oz/319 mL)	crushed pineapple
1 cup (250 mL)	grated raw rutabaga
1 cup (250 mL)	flaked coconut
1/2 cup (125 mL)	pecans
1 tbsp (15 mL)	canola oil
2 tbsp (25 mL)	granulated sugar

GLAZE

1 cup (250 mL)	icing sugar
2 tbsp (25 mL) (approx.)	pineapple juice

For cake: In a large bowl, sift flour, baking soda, baking powder, cinnamon and salt. Set aside.

In a separate bowl, beat eggs until light. Add canola oil, buttermilk, sugar and vanilla and blend well.

Add flour mixture to liquid and mix well. Drain pineapple; set aside juice. Fold in pineapple, rutabaga, coconut and pecans.

Coat a 10-inch (4 L) tube pan with 1 tbsp (15 mL) canola oil and 2 tbsp (25 mL) sugar. Pour mixture into pan.

Bake at 350°F (180°C) for 60 to 65 minutes, or until a tester comes out clean.

Cool in pan for 10 minutes. Turn onto wire rack to complete cooling.

For glaze: Mix icing sugar and pineapple juice. Drizzle over cake.

Bibliography

Daley, Regan. *In the Sweet Kitchen*. Toronto: Random House, 2000.

Davidson, Alan. *The Oxford Companion to Food*. Oxford: Oxford University Press, 1999.

Ferguson, Carol, and Margaret Fraser. *A Century of Canadian Home Cooking: 1900 through the 90s*. Scarborough: Prentice Hall Canada, Inc., 1992.

Levy Beranbaum, Rose. *The Cake Bible*. New York: William Morrow and Company, Inc., 1988.

Mongrain-Dontigny, Micheline. *Traditional Quebec Cooking: A Treasure of Heirloom Recipes*. Montreal: Les Editions La Bonne Recette, 1995.

Morton, Mark. *Cupboard Love: A Dictionary of Culinary Curiosities*. Winnipeg: Bain & Cox, Publishers, an imprint of Blizzard Publishing, 1996.

Murray, Rose. *Rose Murray's Comfortable Kitchen Cookbook*. Toronto: McGraw-Hill Ryerson Limited, 1991.

Nightengale, Marie. *Out of Old Nova Scotia Kitchens*. Nimbus Publishing Limited, 1989.

Powers, Jo Marie, and Anita Stewart. *Northern Bounty: A Celebration of Canadian Cuisine*. Toronto: Random House of Canada, Limited, 1995.

Rombauer, Irma S., Marion Rombauer Becker, and Ethan Becker. *The All New All Purpose Joy of Cooking*. New York: Scribner, 1997.

Scott, Anna Lee. *Cooking Secrets for the Users of Monarch Flour*. Toronto: Maple Leaf Milling Company, Southam Press Toronto, Limited, 1934.

Staebler, Edna. *More Food That Really Schmecks*. Toronto: McClelland and Stewart Limited, 1979.

Stevenson, Lorraine. *Kitchen Culture: Recipes from the 1940s, 50s and 60s*. Winnipeg: *The Manitoba Co-operator*, 1999.

Toussaint-Samat, Maguelonne. *History of Food*. Malden, Massachusetts: Blackwell Publishers, 1992.

Traill, Catherine Parr. *The Canadian Settler's Guide*. Toronto: n.p., 1855.

Purity Cookbook: 875 Tested Recipes. Toronto: Purity Flour Mills Limited, 1932, 1945.

The Five Roses Cook Book. Lake of the Woods Milling Company Limited, n.d.

Tried, Tested, Proved: The Home Cook Book. Compiled by Ladies of Toronto and Chief Cities and Towns in Canada. Toronto: Rose Publishing Company, 1877.

Index